Sacrifice of Self

NAHANT AND THE CIVIL WAR

NAHANT HISTORICAL SOCIETY

Sacrifice of Self

NAHANT AND THE CIVIL WAR

BY STEVEN C. EAMES

[signature]

To Donna Lee Hanlon
I hope you enjoy it!.

Steve

THE
DONNING COMPANY
PUBLISHERS

dedication

to AUSTIN W. BREWIN
WILLIAM M. TWISS

for their concept and hard work

to CALANTHA SEARS

for her perseverance and patience

to ANN RILEY

for her life

*long and hard for her, but it provided
the necessary element for all historical
undertakings—Curiosity*

to KATHLEEN

*for her life, which has always
and will always brighten and
enhance my own*

Photograph, William
M. Twiss (left)
and Austin W.
Brewin at the Civil
War monument
in Greenlawn
Cemetery, Nahant,
ca. early 1990s.
Nahant Historical
Society.

In addition to those mentioned in the author's preface, the Nahant Historical Society gratefully acknowledges the work of the following individuals and organizations that made *Sacrifice of Self* possible.

The late Phillip J. Applin

Catherine S. Bishop

The late Elsie S. Davis

Linda S. Eveleigh and Gretchen R. Sterenberg

Rodney L. Hood Sr.

Edith E. Hunnewell

Mr. and Mrs. Winthrop Donnison Hodges Jr.

Anita Israel, archivist, National Park Service, Longfellow National Historic Site, Cambridge, Massachusetts

Susan E. Keats, vice president of corporate archives and records, Fidelity Investments, Boston

Joseph M. Klink

The late Joseph P. Lermond

The Library of Congress

Robert Mathias, building manager, Grand Army of the Republic Museum, Lynn, Massachusetts

Nahant Public Library

acknowledgments

The late Stanley C. Paterson

Reference Services Branch, National Archives and Records Service, Washington, D.C.

Judith A. Robidoux

The late Carl G. Seaburg

Lynne M. Spencer

Diane Shephard, archivist/librarian, Lynn Museum and Historical Society, Lynn, Massachusetts

The U.S. Navy Historical Center, Washington, D.C.

Robert A. Wilson, Collage Works

Published through the generosity of Ralph Lowell Jr.

Thanks to Bay State Historical League and the Massachusetts Foundation for the Humanities

The Donning Company Publishers
184 Business Park Drive, Suite 206
Virginia Beach, VA 23462

Steve Mull, General Manager
Barbara Buchanan, Office Manager
Pamela Koch, Editor
Amanda D. Guilmain, Graphic Designer
Derek Eley, Imaging Artist
Susan Adams, Project Research Coordinator
Scott Rule, Director of Marketing
Tonya Hannink, Marketing Coordinator

Mary Taylor, Project Director

_____

Library of Congress Cataloging-in-Publication Data

Eames, Steven C., 1954-
  Sacrifice of self : Nahant and the Civil War / by Steven C. Eames.
     p. cm.
  Includes bibliographical references and index.
  ISBN-13: 978-1-57864-405-6 (soft cover : alk. paper)
  ISBN-10: 1-57864-405-4 (soft cover : alk. paper)
  1. Nahant (Mass.)--History, Military--19th century. 2. Massachusetts--History--Civil
War, 1861-1865. 3. Soldiers--Massachusetts--Nahant--History--19th century. I. Title.
  F74.N13E23 2007
  974.4'03--dc22
                              2006037098

Printed in the United States of America at Walsworth Publishing Company

Title page: Map of Nahant from A Topographic Map of Essex County, based on the Trigonometrical Survey of the State. The details for actual survey under the direction of H. F. Wallace, Superintendent of State Map, ca.1856. Published by Smith and Morley, 106 Washington Street, Boston, and engraved and manufactured by R. P. Smith Map Establishment, Philadelphia. Nahant Historical Society.

contents

Two members of the Nahant, Massachusetts, Historical Society, the late Austin W. Brewin and William M. Twiss, conceived this project. These two men took it upon themselves to discover all that they could about the men from Nahant who served in the Civil War. They did not restrict their effort to residents of the town in the 1860s. They investigated anyone connected to the town, in any way possible, who performed military service. This was certainly a "labor of love," but somehow the use of this cliché is inadequate to describe their quest. Austin and William spent a tremendous amount of energy and explored many avenues to accumulate the necessary information. They contacted agencies in Washington, D.C., they traveled to other towns, and they wrote letters. Faced with a shopping bag full of replies and handwritten notes, they set about to organize and type the information.

Once they had the information, however, they could not or would not proceed. They were not professional writers or historians, and truth be told, they were uncomfortable with some of the information they uncovered and feared they might hurt some descendants. (Actually, I found little that was negative, so I suspect they may have misinterpreted some of it.) Into the picture now stepped Calantha Sears, curator of the Nahant Historical Society. She knew what to do: organize the information, publish it, and refuse to let that tremendous labor languish. She sought a grant and contacted me to put it together. During the project, she tirelessly tracked down obscure information. Her voice on the phone spurred me on.

preface

There are so many people who help in such a project, and too few get
proper acknowledgment. I want to thank the late Stanley Paterson
for his suggestions and the loan of his Longfellow and Palfry family
material. Steve Schier, curator of the Lynn GAR Hall, proved a great
help and an excellent tour guide. Ken Turino, formerly of the Lynn
Historical Society, provided valuable suggestions after reading the
first draft, and the late Phillip Applin worked hard to track down
the Greenlawn burial records. Daniel A. deStefano and Suzanne M.
Hamill served as invaluable editors, and Bonnie Ayers D'Orlando
provided crucial effort to keep the project going. My wife, Kathleen,
as always, has been supportive, bucking me up when down and taking
over more than her share of the household chores. And my children?
Well, they are wonderful, and I love them very much, even if they were
on occasion the cause of delay.

However, the heroes of this work are Austin, William, and Calantha.
While it is true that my name appears on the cover, I was simply an
instrument. I gave *their* story a voice.

one

ANTEBELLUM NAHANT

THIS IS THE STORY OF NAHANT, MASSACHUSETTS, AND THE CIVIL WAR. It is the story of the men who went to war, the community who stayed behind, and the impact of that great conflict on the veterans and the town in the decades that followed Appomattox. In general, this experience is no different from that of thousands of other communities between 1861 and 1865. Men enlisted in the army and went off to war; some were killed and some wounded, but most returned to resume their lives. While they were away, the loved ones, friends, and neighbors did what they could to support their men in the service and "kept the home fires burning" until their return. But generalities obscure character. No two communities are exactly alike for the simple reason that the individuals who make up the communities are unique. The experience of war is also personal and widely varied. The story of Nahant in the Civil War essentially confirms the general concepts, but does so in an uncommon and individual way. The story is much like the town itself, which may be called uniquely familiar.

The first unique aspect about Nahant is its location. Nahant is a peninsula jutting out from Lynn, Massachusetts, north of Boston. For centuries, the precarious moods of nature determined whether Nahant remained two islands or became a peninsula (now it remains so due to strong stone sea walls). Its only link to the mainland ran through Lynn, and so naturally it was part of that town, and the early settlers came from Lynn. The land was first used as pasture only, but by the mid-eighteenth century, three families had established themselves—the Breeds, Hoods, and Johnsons. Samuel Breed, Richard Hood, and

Photographic portrait, The Politics and Poetry of New England: longtime friends Charles Sumner (left) and Henry Wadsworth Longfellow (right). Photographer Alexander Gardner, Washington, D.C., ca. December 8, 1863. Courtesy National Park Service, Longfellow National Historic Site.

Jonathan Johnson can be considered the town fathers, with Hood and Johnson having a direct connection to the Civil War. Richard Hood would beget Abner who would beget Ebenezer who would beget Elbridge who would beget Elbridge G. Hood. Jonathan Johnson, nicknamed "Trooper" because of service in a local mounted unit during the French and Indian Wars, would beget Benjamin, Joseph, and Caleb. Caleb would beget five boys and five girls. Joseph would beget Washington Hervey, Edmund B., and seemingly dozens of others. Benjamin moved to Lynn and was equally prolific.[1]

In the eighteenth century, as in most New England coastal communities, the settlers made their living from the land and the sea, farming and fishing. By the 1790s, they found the number of people coming to Nahant for nature excursions had increased to the point that some individuals offered their houses for replenishment and overnight stays. All three families had members doing this. In this, Nahant anticipated the New England tourist industry by seventy or eighty years. Although not always successful, Nahanters continued to supplement their income by catering to visitors in the summer.[2] The sighting of a sea serpent in 1819 helped business. At the same time, the Boston merchant named "Colonel" Thomas Handasyd Perkins conceived of an idea to build a house that could be lived in during the summer. In 1820, he had the first summer cottage built, moved his daughter, Elizabeth "Eliza," and her husband, Samuel Cabot, into it (with the proviso that he could visit), and began the tradition of "cottagers" or summer residents.[3] Five years later, Frederic Tudor would join the cottagers. Tudor built his stone cottage in the center of the peninsula, and over time, he would contribute greatly to the community. Other wealthy families would follow suit, including the manufacturing Lawrence family. Their numbers grew so much that in 1832 they established their own nondenominational house of worship, the Nahant Church, rotating ministers from a variety of Protestant sects on a weekly basis.[4]

But Colonel Perkins's ideas did not end with the summer cottage. Many people came to Nahant for much shorter stays, so Perkins dreamed up the idea of a hotel. It was a grand structure but not successful at first, so Perkins sold out to another summer cottager, Dr. Edward Robbins, in

1827. Robbins promoted a steamship connection with Boston, making it far easier for the elite to find Nahant and his hotel. Perkins rejoined the business soon after, and the hotel served to expose many people to the natural glories of Nahant.[5] And through it all, the year-round residents, like the Hoods and the prolific Johnsons, continued to farm, fish, and have children. In 1851, they established the Village Church for the year-round residents.[6]

In 1850, the full-time residents of Nahant numbered 198, and 87 of them were Johnsons.[7] By 1850, a second generation of cottagers appeared: people whose fame was less connected to money and more to literature, science, and politics. Among the luminaries were Henry Wadsworth Longfellow, professor of literature at Harvard University; Louis Agassiz, professor of zoology at Harvard; Charles Sumner, soon to be senator from Massachusetts; and the Lodge family, including a young Henry Cabot Lodge.[8] By now, Phineas Drew ran the Nahant Hotel. He found himself constrained by the stringent liquor laws of Lynn, and so he threw his considerable influence behind the cause of separation and independence.

Nahant achieved this independence (and Drew the ability to serve liquor freely) in 1853. Justice of the Peace Welcome W. Johnson, son of Caleb, issued a proper warrant to Washington H. Johnson, son of Joseph, to create the government of a town. Walter Johnson, son of Joseph, was voted in as moderator, and Washington H. Johnson became town clerk. The first three selectmen were William F. Johnson, Dexter

1. Stanley C. Paterson and Carl G. Seaburg, *Nahant on the Rocks* (Nahant Historical Society, 1991), 40–41; Fred A. Wilson, *Some Annals of Nahant, Massachusetts* (Boston, 1928), 44–49.

2. Paterson & Seaburg, *Nahant*, 46.

3. Paterson & Seaburg, *Nahant*, 50–61; Wilson, *Annals*, 160–67.

4. Paterson & Seaburg, *Nahant*, 71–81. Catholics would not be accepted until the 1860s.

5. Paterson & Seaburg, *Nahant*, 64–66; Wilson, *Annals*, 76–79.

6. Paterson & Seaburg, *Nahant*, 90; Wilson, *Annals*, 216–17.

7. Paterson & Seaburg, *Nahant*, 103.

8. Paterson & Seaburg, *Nahant*, 86–95.

Stetson, and Artemus Murdock. Welcome W. Johnson became treasurer and served on the school committee along with Walter Johnson and John Hammond. They also chose all those other officers so necessary for a town at the time—the field drivers, fence viewer, surveyor of highways, and surveyor of lumber. They decided March would be the time of their annual meeting.[9]

In 1853, they drew up a list of men eligible for the militia. The list had forty-three names, including seventeen Johnsons. Throughout the 1850s, Massachusetts militia regiments, including the Fifth and the Eighth, occasionally used Nahant as their summer training camp. The following year, Washington H. Johnson won election to selectman and would serve on that body for twenty-three years, through the Civil War and well into the postwar period.[10]

By the mid-1850s, the new town of Nahant had achieved a comfortable balance. The population was a mixture of year-round farmers and fishermen and part-time poets, Boston Brahmins, and Harvard professors. All accepted each other. The records reveal little of the animosity toward "summer people" that often is evident today in other areas of New England. The summer cottagers and hotel owners contributed to the community, and the year-round residents welcomed them with open arms, especially as in some cases they were relatives. The picture that comes down to us often was painted by the summer people. We should be aware that they came to escape the hubbub of their normal lives, but it is a picture of calm and natural beauty. We can see this in one passage from Longfellow's journal when he observed that "one of the prettiest sights of Nahant is the cows going over the beach at sunset, from the cow-rights of Nahant to the cow-yards of Lynn. Their red hides, and the reflection in the wet sand light up the gray picture of the sky and surge."[11] Picturesque, idyllic, peaceful—all that would change in the 1860s with the coming of war.

9. Paterson & Seaburg, *Nahant*, 103–4; Wilson, *Annals*, 254–59.

10. Paterson & Seaburg, *Nahant*, 123–25; Wilson, *Annals*, 259–60.

11. Samuel Longfellow, ed., *Life of Henry Wadsworth Longfellow with extracts from his Journals and Correspondence* (1891; reprinted NY 1969), Vol. II, 187.

ENCAMPMENT OF THE BOSTON CADETS, AT NAHANT.

It is not the purpose of this study to argue the causes of the Civil War nor relate all the events and issues that led to the secession of the South and the firing on Fort Sumter; however, some sort of succinct reminder is necessary. Essentially the Civil War was an identity crisis—the identity crisis of a nation born in 1776, grown to adolescence, and faced with the decision finally of what it would be. Would the United States become forward looking and embrace industry, with all the consequences that industrialization entailed, or would the country remain an agricultural society, supported by slavery?

This crisis was implanted at birth. As with many children, the new nation had parents with hopes and dreams for their future, in this case two fathers—Thomas Jefferson and Alexander Hamilton. Both chose

Line engraving, "Encampment of the Boston Cadets, at Nahant," *Gleason's Pictorial Drawing Room Companion*, August 9, 1851. Nahant Historical Society.

career paths for their offspring. For Hamilton, the country's future lay along the path taken by Great Britain—industrial power and a strong central government. Jefferson felt just the opposite. Farmers were the backbone of America, and farmers needed no central control. The central government was necessary but must be small, its authority held in check by the sovereign power of the states. The battle between these two visions would be fought out in the writing of the Constitution and Bill of Rights and would lead to the formation of political parties— surrogate parents who would carry on the fight after the fathers had passed away. Political parties would be the little voices in the conscience of the new nation, whispering their advice to go this way or that.

Slavery was the issue that forced the decision. This iniquitous practice existed before the birth of the new nation and became an ugly birth defect after, inflicting emotional and physical pain to the human beings under its control and twisting the thoughts and beliefs of all it touched. But slavery defined and supported the agricultural community of the South. Agriculture meant the growing of a staple crop, first tobacco and then cotton. This was accomplished most efficiently on large plantations, with black slaves to perform all the labor, at least in the opinion of the plantation owners. The "Great Planters" actually made up a very small percentage of the southern population, but they held complete economic, political, and social control. Jefferson might have said that a true republican was a man with a hoe and a hundred acres, but it is doubtful the planter class of the South ever touched a hoe. Agriculture did not evoke images of the family farm like it did in the North—the idyllic vision of Longfellow and the red cows of Nahant. Agriculture to the planter class was big business. The cotton they grew fed the mills of Old England and New England; it pumped money into the economy of the South, and it enabled the planters to maintain their feudal lifestyle.

However, the planters lived on credit. They were always in debt. Their elegance was based on money borrowed from the merchants they sold to and secured with the promise of future crops. Their real capital was sunk into land and slaves. In their minds, the land was not worth anything without the slaves to work it. So even an enlightened man like Thomas Jefferson could hate the concept and practice of slavery yet own slaves all his life, dying with a debt of $100,000. Although he tried to convince himself and everyone else that he held on to his slaves because he was worried about their welfare, the simple fact was that Jefferson was a slave himself to an economic system. To free his slaves would have brought him personal economic ruin and would have done very little to end slavery. No single individual could end slavery; slavery had to be destroyed by the nation.

In the political system established under the Constitution, power rested on numbers. In the House of Representatives, it was population, in the Senate, the number of states. Even counting three-fifths of the slaves under the Constitution's Three-Fifths Compromise, the South could never hope to equal the growing urban population of the North and so early on surrendered any hope in the House. However, as long as the number of slave and free states remained equal in the Senate, the South could protect its "peculiar institution." So it was the expansion of the country westward, and thus the creation of more states, that brought the issue into focus. It began with the Missouri Compromise of 1820, a crisis that Jefferson called a "fire bell in the night" warning of the destruction of the nation, and grew into an open sore after the Mexican War when the United States gained (or grabbed, depending on one's outlook) vast new territory in the west, territory that would become new states. The increasingly vexing and even brutal question was, would these states be slave or free? This concerned the South even more by the 1850s because of a very vocal minority in the North that had embarked on a holy crusade to destroy slavery.

The Abolitionist Movement began in the 1830s. Simply put (and that is all we have time for), it grew out of the new Romantic thinking. Unlike the Enlightenment of the eighteenth century, whose thinkers believed everything on earth belonged to the "Great Chain of Being" and thus had to be accepted (including slavery), Romantic thinkers believed in change and motion. They did not look on society and nature and see "things as they are," but they saw "things as they will become." From such thought came concepts of evolution and extinction. Slavery in America was a brutality. It involved the control and degradation of human beings. Dominance came from convincing slaves of their inferiority and providing constant reminders and demonstrations of the control masters had over them. It involved racism—the cultivated belief that blacks were inferior human beings and thus needed to be controlled. Indeed, many slave owners believed that because of this innate incapacity blacks actually benefited from slavery. Abolitionists wanted to make this abhorrent system extinct.

The abolitionists, in their virulent attacks on the institution, threatened the Southern planter way of life and his economic well-being, particularly as the abolitionists in America never believed in the compensation of slave owners for the loss of their property, a system England had used to abolish slavery in its empire peacefully. Even more than that, the abolitionists intended to turn loose the people that the planters had degraded, shamed, whipped, raped, and dominated for two hundred years. The Southern planters could not let this happen.

The future development of the territory gained after the Mexican War opened the wounds once again. The 1850s lurched from one crisis to the next. The South used the political system to its advantage, pushing through the Fugitive Slave Law and favorable Supreme Court rulings, and in each case the North flouted the law,[12] even to the point of fostering armed slave insurrection (John Brown's raid at Harper's Ferry). More and more abolitionists won election to Congress, including Nahant's summer visitor Charles Sumner. Sumner was vocal in his opposition to the expansion of slavery, and in 1856, he was beaten with a cane while sitting at his senate seat by South Carolina's Representative Preston Brooks.

As their attempts to force the North to accept laws and judicial rulings failed and their prospects of gaining more slave states to preserve the balance in the Senate dimmed with each passing year, the South turned increasingly to the concept of "States' Rights" to defend slavery and their way of life. This view, dating back to the birth of the nation, characterized the Constitution as a league of sovereign states. The ultimate political power rested in the individual states, and the central government was simply a convenient way to coordinate efforts for foreign affairs and trade, much like the United Nations is today. As articulated by Thomas Jefferson in the Kentucky Resolution of 1799, states had the right to "nullify" federal laws, to declare them void within the boundaries of the state, and if the central government attempted to force states to comply, this broke the contract and the state had the right to withdraw from the compact, just as the United States today has the right to withdraw from the United Nations if it wishes.

By 1860, many in the South had determined that the time for withdrawal had come, and the political leaders of South Carolina declared that if a Republican, the party of the abolitionists, was elected president, they would withdraw that state from the Union. When the word reached them in December that Abraham Lincoln had been elected, South Carolina called a state convention and voted to secede. The other states in the Deep South quickly followed, and the country held its breath to see how the new president would respond. When Lincoln attempted to send supplies to Fort Sumter in Charleston, South Carolina, the Southern forces opened fire on the fort on April 12, 1861. Abraham Lincoln called for seventy-five thousand militia to put down the rebellion. The states in the upper South refused to provide men to fight their own, and they quickly seceded as well to join their brethren in the Deep South. The Civil War had begun.

It is difficult to know how Nahanters felt during the procession of events in the 1850s. For most people in the North, the issue of secession did not concern the fate of the slaves (abolitionists were a minority, and racism existed in the North as well). They saw the South destroying the great nation created in the blood and fire of the Revolution. The Constitution was a compact of the American people, not the states. The identity crisis had led to a suicide attempt. The South would kill the nation to win its argument, and people in the North were determined to prevent this at all costs. Longfellow recorded his feelings in his journal. On February 15, 1861, he wrote, "the dissolution of the Union goes

12. Boston provided two famous incidents in opposition to the Fugitive Slave Law.

Photograph, ca. 1880, the Nahant Volunteer Militia led by Captain Luther Dame drilled behind this 1851 wooden schoolhouse, located on what is now Pleasant Street and a children's playground. Used as both a school and town hall, the schoolhouse was razed in 1905 when the brick Valley Road School on the south side of town, now the Society's home, was completed. Nahant Historical Society.

slowly on. Behind it all I hear the low murmur of the slaves, like a chorus in a Greek tragedy, prophesying woe! woe!"[13] On April 12, he learned the South had pulled the trigger. "News comes that Fort Sumter is attacked. And so the war begins! Who can foresee the end?"[14]

It seems likely from their reaction that the people of Nahant shared the feelings of most northerners. On April 23, the town held a special meeting in the vestry of the Village Church on Nahant Road. The most important order of business was the formation of a military company dubbed the "Home Guard." Luther Dame, teacher at the elementary school, was named the captain, and nearly all the able-bodied men signed up. Images of the Massachusetts Minutemen of the American War for Independence must have flashed through their minds. The Home Guard members bought their own uniforms, and a subscription raised the funds for weapons. Luther Dame had his company drilling behind the school several evenings each week.[15]

It all seemed so exciting and so worthwhile. As the Home Guard drilled, the militia regiments called up by the president began to leave for Washington. On April 19, the anniversary of Lexington and Concord, the Sixth Massachusetts Militia found themselves fighting in the city of Baltimore through a crowd of Southern sympathizers. Shots were exchanged, and men died. It was a sad affair to be sure, but some deaths in war were to be expected. If only Americans in the spring of 1861 had known what was to come.

---

13. *Life of Longfellow*, Vol. II, 412.

14. *Life of Longfellow*, Vol. II, 414.

15. Wilson, *Annals*, 103.

two

NAHANT GOES TO WAR

THE FIRST NAHANT RESIDENT TO SERVE WAS ALREADY IN THE MILITARY when the war began, and he would finish with probably the most illustrious career of all the resident Nahanters. Mortimer Laurence Johnson was born in Nahant in 1842 and attended primary school in the community and high school in Lynn. Johnson easily passed the examinations and received an appointment to the Naval Academy in 1860.[1] However, his course of study would be short. Like the West Pointers who were graduated early at the start of the war, nineteen-year-old Mortimer Johnson was plucked from Annapolis by the Navy and assigned as a midshipman on the *Susquehanna* in May 1861. He would serve that ship until August and then, in order, the frigates *Sabine* and *Wabash*. These ships were attached to the South Atlantic Squadron operating in the Charleston area. On September 11, 1862, he was promoted to ensign and fought at St. John's Bluff, Florida, capturing the enemy's flag. He was promoted to lieutenant in February 1864. From August 1864 to January 1865, he served on the steam frigate *Colorado* and participated in both attacks on Fort Fisher, North Carolina. The first attack occurred the end of December 1864; the second and more successful attack took place in mid-January 1865. Mortimer Johnson distinguished himself during these attacks. In his official report, Commodore Henry Knox Thatcher wrote, "I have to commend to your notice, for the bravery especially Lieutenant M. L. Johnson, who, in the midst of a heavy fire from the enemy, with a boat's crew of volunteers, carried a boat's hawser from the ship [the *Colorado*] to the *New Ironsides* in order to enable us to bring all the guns to bear from the port battery and was, for more than a half an hour, the target

Carte de visite, ca. October 1862. Although his training at Annapolis was cut short by the war, Ensign Mortimer Laurence Johnson was a bright and able naval officer retiring finally as rear admiral and commandant of Boston Navy Yard. Courtesy of Nahant Public Library.

for the forts to which they availed themselves, fortunately, without success."[2] Johnson also participated in a landing action where he received a wound in the leg and apparently captured a small enemy flag.[3]

After Fort Fisher, Johnson became a flag lieutenant of the West Gulf Squadron and commanded the *Estrella*. At the war's conclusion, he was posted to the Pacific. Promoted to lieutenant commander in July 1868, Johnson lived the usual wandering life of the military. He served on ships on European and Asiatic stations, and he did duty at both the Portsmouth and Boston Navy Yards. He received his captaincy in 1893 and commanded the *Franklin* (1894–95) and the *Cincinnati* (1895–97). On leave at the outbreak of the Spanish-American War, Johnson requested active service and was given command of the double-turreted monitor *Miantanomoh* and operated with the fleet around Cuba. After the war, he became executive officer of the Boston Navy Yard. On January 29, 1901, he was promoted to rear admiral and first hoisted his flag over Port Royal, South Carolina. His service there was short,

1. The biographical information comes from the research done by Austin W. Brewin and William M. Twiss. Brewin and Twiss used numerous sources, including pension records, obituaries, and government papers, to document the lives of the men associated with Nahant in the Civil War. I have relied on their research in the preparation of this and other chapters, confirmed most of it, and corrected the few errors made. The information is typed, organized alphabetically, and readily available. The file is located in the Nahant Historical Society archives and labeled "Soldiers Biographies" (hereafter cited as "Soldier Bio" file, NHS).

2. Lynn *Daily Evening Item*, February 15, 1913, Johnson obituary.

3. The flag is now at the Nahant Historical Society.

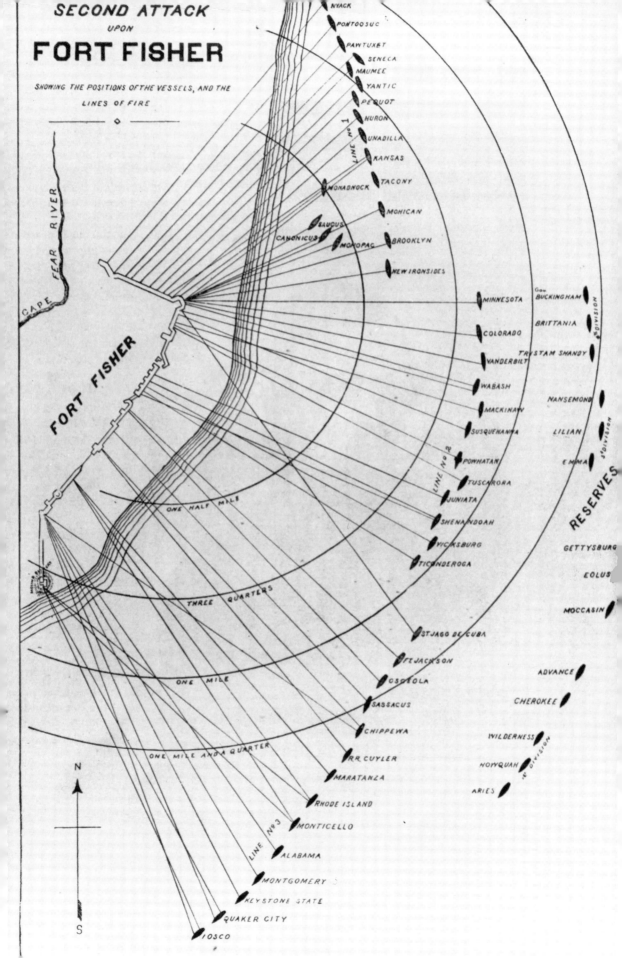

SECOND ATTACK
UPON
FORT FISHER

SHOWING THE POSITIONS OF THE VESSELS, AND THE
LINES OF FIRE

CAPE FEAR RIVER

FORT FISHER

NYACK
PONTOOSUC
PAWTUXET
SENECA
MAUMEE
YANTIC
PEQUOT
HURON
UNADILLA
KANSAS
TACONY
MOHICAN
SAUGUS
CANONICUS
MONADNOCK
MONOPAC
BROOKLYN
NEW IRONSIDES

LINE Nº 1

MINNESOTA
COLORADO
VANDERBILT
WABASH
MACKINAW
SUSQUEHANNA
POWHATAN
TUSCARORA
JUNIATA
SHENANDOAH
VICKSBURG
TICONDEROGA

LINE Nº 2

ONE HALF MILE

THREE QUARTERS

ONE MILE

ONE MILE AND A QUARTER

STJAGO DE CUBA
FT JACKSON
OSCEOLA
SASSACUS
CHIPPEWA
RR CUYLER
MARATANZA
RHODE ISLAND
MONTICELLO
ALABAMA
MONTGOMERY
KEYSTONE STATE
QUAKER CITY
IOSCO

LINE Nº 3

Gov BUCKINGHAM
BRITTANIA
TRISTAM SHANDY
NANSEMOND
LILIAN
EMMA

RESERVES

GETTYSBURG
EOLUS
MOCCASIN
ADVANCE
CHEROKEE
WILDERNESS
HOWQUAH
ARIES

N
S

and by the end of the year, he was back in Boston as commandant of the Navy Yard, a post he held until his retirement in 1904. This proved to be a very distinguished career for the only Nahant resident from the Civil War to stay in the military.

For the rest of Nahant's Civil War soldiers, the years 1861–65 would be their only military experience. Following the attack on Fort Sumter, Abraham Lincoln called into service seventy-five thousand militia for three months, all the time the current law would allow. Lincoln and his government understood that this militia call-up would only buy time, and more soldiers would be needed. On May 3, 1861, they issued the first order for three-year volunteers (forty regiments) and continued to recruit throughout the rest of 1861. None of the Nahant men served with the ninety-day militia units, but several joined three-year volunteer regiments during 1861.[4]

The next Nahant resident to answer the call of arms, beside the service of Luther Dame in the Home Guard, was William L. Rand. The twenty-five-year-old Rand joined the Twelfth Massachusetts Volunteer Infantry on June 26, 1861, and, excepting Mortimer Johnson, Rand served longer than any other Nahant resident. Indeed, his participation and dedication to the war effort makes his story even more poignant.

The Twelfth Massachusetts was called the "Webster Regiment" because the man who raised it and would serve as its first colonel was Fletcher Webster, son of Daniel Webster. The Twelfth was mustered into federal service in June 1861 and first saw active service in the Shenandoah Valley under General Nathaniel Banks in the spring of 1862. Later that summer, they were assigned to McDowell's Corps, Army of Virginia,

---

4. Francis A. Lord, *They Fought for the Union* (New York, 1960), 1–2.

and fought at Cedar Mountain and Second Bull Run. Colonel Fletcher Webster died in the latter battle. Next assigned to Hooker's Corps, the Twelfth marched into the cornfield on the morning of September 17 at the start of the Battle of Antietam. They captured the colors of the First Texas and lost 224 killed and wounded, among the latter, William Rand. The wound was apparently slight because Rand returned to the regiment in time for their next battle, Fredericksburg, where he was wounded again.

The Twelfth continued to serve in the Army of the Potomac, at Chancellorsville and Gettysburg in 1863, and the Wilderness and Spotsylvania in May of 1864. On January 1, 1864, William Rand took advantage of the bounty offered by the federal government and reenlisted. When the original three-year enlistments of the Twelfth Massachusetts ran out in June 1864, the recent recruits and reenlisted men (including William Rand) were transferred to the Thirty-ninth Massachusetts. Now with the Thirty-ninth, William Rand experienced the siege of Petersburg through 1864 and into 1865. Then his luck ran out. He was killed on March 31, 1865, in a small battle at White Oak Road. Among the first batch of three-year enlistments, Rand committed himself long term even before the First Battle of Bull Run. He served for almost four years, was wounded twice, and died in battle ten days before Robert E. Lee surrendered.[5]

Following closely after Rand, John Henry Gray Hood enlisted on August 29, 1861, and joined Company B of the Seventh Kansas Cavalry on September 16. Hood had grown up on Nahant and moved to Berlin, Illinois, just before the war began. He rose to sergeant by 1863 and served throughout the war, mustering out in September 1865. The Seventh Kansas was known as "Jennison's Jayhawkers" and early in the war served in the brutal district of western Missouri and then Kansas. In 1862, the regiment reported to Mississippi and was placed in a brigade commanded by Colonel Philip H. Sheridan. Company B participated in the battle of Iuka, Mississippi, on September 18, 1862. The regiment then participated in the Battle of Corinth on October 4, 1862. The Seventh joined General Ulysses S. Grant's command and was involved

5. "Soldier Bio" file, NHS; Adjutant-General's Office, *Massachusetts Soldiers, Sailors and Marines in the Civil War* (Boston, 1932; hereafter listed as *Mass. Soldiers*). Regimental histories and rosters are presented in numerical order. See report on 12th and 39th Massachusetts Volunteer Infantry.

in numerous expeditions and small engagements with the rebels. In
1864, the Seventh Kansas participated in the campaign against the
rebel general Sterling Price. It ended the war fighting guerrillas in
Missouri and was mustered out of service on September 29, 1865.[6]

William J. Johnson (no relation to the larger Johnson family at
Nahant) joined the Twenty-fourth Massachusetts Volunteer Infantry,
which was mustered into service in September 1861. The Twenty-
fourth became part of General Ambrose Burnside's Coast Division and
participated in the capture of Roanoke, Virginia, February 8, 1862,
and New Bern, North Carolina, March 14, 1862. The Twenty-fourth
remained in the Carolinas, serving in the Goldsboro Expedition in
December 1862 (see next chapter) and in the attacks on Charleston.
William J. Johnson mustered out of the regiment as a sergeant on
July 3, 1863.[7]

Another resident, Alfred A. Tarbox, also joined the army in September
1861. He enlisted in the Twenty-second Massachusetts but was
discharged for disability on January 1, 1862. Tarbox later served with
the Eighth Massachusetts Militia during its nine-month service from

6. Kansas Historical Society, *http://www.kshs.org/genealogists/military
/7thks.htm*; Ancestry.com, John H. G. Hood, Kansas Civil War Soldiers Records,
http://search.ancestry.com.

7. "Soldier Bio" file, NHS; *Mass. Soldiers*, 24th Mass. Vol. Inf.

September 1862 to July 1863. During that time, the Eighth served at New Bern, North Carolina, where its companies were broken up for various outpost duties.[8]

On October 12, 1861, Irish immigrant and town resident Patrick Riley left his pregnant wife Ann, two children, and his mother to enlist in Company A, Twenty-eighth Massachusetts Volunteer Infantry. The Twenty-eighth was an Irish regiment, known officially as the Second Irish Regiment (the first was the Ninth Massachusetts), and was raised at the urging not only of local Irish leaders, but also of Thomas Meagher, who wanted it for the Irish Brigade he was then forming. The original members of Company A came almost exclusively from Lynn, commanded by Captain Andrew Carraher.

The Twenty-eighth mustered into federal service on December 13, 1861 (Riley as a corporal), and left Massachusetts the end of January 1862. Although raised with Meagher's Irish Brigade in mind, the Twenty-eighth Massachusetts would not be assigned there initially. Instead, it was sent to the expedition threatening Charleston, South Carolina. The Twenty-eighth fought its first battle at Secessionville on James Island on June 16, 1862. Then it joined General John

Pope's Army of Virginia and participated in the Second Battle of Bull Run, August 29–30. Two days later, the regiment fought in the Battle of Chantilly. Known mostly for the death of General Philip Kearny, the engagement was fought in a wild, blinding thunderstorm. The Twenty-eighth Massachusetts suffered one hundred casualties, among them Patrick Riley. Riley never recovered from his wound and died in a hospital in Alexandria, Virginia, on December 1, 1862.[9]

Photograph. John Henry Gray Hood, shown in old age, ca. 1900, was the elder brother of Elbridge Gerry Hood and served with the Seventh Cavalry in the western theater of the war. Nahant Historical Society.

8. *Mass. Soldiers*, 8th Mass. Militia.

After serving as captain of the Home Guard Company, Luther Dame was commissioned captain of the Third Unattached Company on October 12, 1861. Unattached companies were raised for short terms, in this case ninety days, and filled local garrison functions. Dame would later be commissioned a captain in Company G, Eleventh Massachusetts Volunteer Infantry, but his service would be short. Commissioned on September 8, 1863, he would not be mustered (or confirmed in rank) until May 13, 1864, and would leave the regiment two months later.[10]

Another connection to the Eleventh Massachusetts was George F. Newhall. This thirty-year-old gardener left his wife and four children to enlist in the Eleventh on December 28, 1861. The Eleventh Massachusetts served in General Joseph Hooker's division, Third Corps, in the Peninsula Campaign, fighting at Williamsburg and Fair Oaks. The regiment also fought at Second Bull Run where it led its brigade in the assault on Stonewall Jackson's position along the famous unfinished railroad bed. Close hand-to-hand combat led to a break in the line, but they were unsupported, and a rebel counterattack eventually drove them back. The Eleventh Massachusetts lost 112, including 28 killed or mortally wounded. George F. Newhall was among the dead.[11]

By the beginning of 1862, the government had over six hundred thousand volunteers in service and came to the erroneous conclusion that this mighty force would suffice to end the rebellion. Consequently, orders were issued on April 3, 1862, to close recruiting stations throughout the north and to return the recruiting officers to their regiments for the start of the campaign season. The shocking casualty rates from the Battle of Shiloh and George McClellan's Peninsula Campaign soon illustrated how short-sighted this had been. Recruiting offices were reopened on June 6, and on July 2, the War Department called for three hundred thousand more three-

Title page, *Practical Navigator* by Nathaniel Bowditch, 1864—A vital navigational resource for the United States Navy. Nahant Historical Society.

9. "Soldier Bio" file, NHS; *Mass. Soldiers*, 28th Mass. Vol. Inf.; D. P. Conyngham, *The Irish Brigade and Its Campaigns* (Boston, 1869; reprinted Gaithersburg, MD, 1987), 576–89; Nahant Town Census, 1860 & 1865, Nahant Historical Society.

10. "Soldier Bio" file, NHS; *Mass. Soldiers*, 11th Mass. Vol. Inf.

11. "Soldier Bio" file, NHS; *Mass. Soldiers*, 11th Mass. Vol. Inf.; John J. Hennessy, *Return to Bull Run: The Campaign and Battle of Second Manassas* (New York, 1993), 248–57.

THE

NEW AMERICAN
PRACTICAL NAVIGATOR:

BEING AN

EPITOME OF NAVIGATION,

CONTAINING

ALL THE TABLES

NECESSARY TO BE USED WITH THE NAUTICAL ALMANAC IN

DETERMINING THE LATITUDE AND THE LONGITUDE

BY LUNAR OBSERVATIONS,

AND KEEPING A COMPLETE RECKONING AT SEA;

ILLUSTRATED BY PROPER RULES AND EXAMPLES:

THE WHOLE EXEMPLIFIED IN A JOURNAL KEPT FROM BOSTON TO MADEIRA, IN WHICH

ALL THE RULES OF NAVIGATION ARE INTRODUCED ;

ALSO,

THE DEMONSTRATION OF THE USUAL RULES OF TRIGONOMETRY ; PROB
LEMS IN MENSURATION, SURVEYING, AND GAUGING.

WITH AN APPENDIX,

CONTAINING METHODS OF CALCULATING ECLIPSES OF THE SUN AND MOON, AND OCCULTATIONS OF
THE FIXED STARS; RULES FOR FINDING THE LONGITUDE OF A PLACE BY OBSERVATIONS OF
ECLIPSES, OCCULTATIONS, AND TRANSITS OF THE MOON'S LIMB OVER THE MERIDIAN;
ALSO, A NEW METHOD FOR FINDING THE LATITUDE BY TWO ALTITUDES.

BY NATHANIEL BOWDITCH, LL. D.,

*Fellow of the Royal Societies of London, Edinburgh, and Dublin ; of the Astronomical Society in London ; of
the American Philosophical Society, held at Philadelphia ; of the American Academy of Arts and
Sciences ; of the Connecticut Academy of Arts and Sciences ; of the Literary and Philosophical Society of New-York ; Corresponding Member of the Royal Societies of Berlin,
Palermo, &c.,—and since his decease, continued by his son,*

J. INGERSOLL BOWDITCH.

THIRTY-SECOND NEW STEREOTYPE EDITION.

NEW-YORK:

PUBLISHED BY E. & G. W. BLUNT, PROPRIETORS,
No. 179 WATER STREET, CORNER OF BURLING SLIP.

1864.

year volunteers.[12] Many have agreed that this crop of volunteers was probably among the best raised during the war, mainly because they did not enlist with wild romantic notions but with the grim determination of men who knew of the slaughter on the battlefield and yet understood their duty.

On July 14, Congress passed a law enabling the president to call out the militia for nine months instead of ninety days. Lincoln followed through on August 4, calling out three hundred thousand militia for nine-month service (this was in addition to the three hundred thousand called out for three-year volunteer service). To fill this order for six hundred thousand men, two methods were used: quotas and bounties. Quotas were assigned to the states, which in turn apportioned the responsibility to individual towns. This was not a draft, although similar in intent. Communities were obligated to send a

Painting, USS *Estrella* (at the left) off the Pensacola Navy Yard, Florida c.1862–67, Mortimer Johnson commanded this 438-ton "burden" side-wheel steamship late in the war. USS *Yucca* is in the middle distance. The sailing frigate at right is not identified. Courtesy of U.S. Naval Historical Center, Photo # NH 380.

certain number of men. Who they sent and how they got them was up to the community. Bounties were substantial payments as rewards for enlistment. The federal government provided a $100 bounty for all three-year volunteers, and the states and even local communities provided bounties as well. This not only encouraged residents, but also many communities allowed men to be "credited" to the town when going into the service. These nonresidents collected the local bounty and helped fill the town's quota.[13]

Nahant's recruiting pattern in 1862 reflects these developments. The only resident to enlist between December of 1861 and June of 1862 was Charles Warren Johnson. The thirty-eight-year-old gardener joined the navy on March 13. He served on the *Ohio*, then the

12. A total of 421,465 actually volunteered at this call.

13. Lord, *They Fought for the Union*, 2–4.

Maratanza, and died on July 20, 1862, at the U.S. Naval Hospital at Norfolk, Virginia.[14] Recruiting did not pick up until after Lincoln's call for three hundred thousand volunteers in early July, but the next three months brought the largest group of enlistments connected to Nahant during the whole war. According to the *Annals of Nahant*, a town meeting was held on July 19 "to see what action the town will take in relation to raising the town's quota of volunteers in response to the call of the Governor of this Commonwealth." At the annual town meeting in March, the town had voted for a $200 bounty for soldiers who enlisted. Now some wealthy residents, both full- and part-time, offered more money to willing recruits. John E. Lodge offered $25 to the first seven, and James W. Paige offered the same to the first four. Nathaniel Walker picked up the tab for the remaining three, and then Frederic Tudor offered $25 for the whole quota.[15]

Three residents went into the Thirty-fifth Massachusetts Volunteer Infantry; William H. Hanson, a heeler, enlisted on July 24 and John Wheeler, another heeler, the next day. Both were in Company D. Elbridge Gerry Hood (younger brother of John Henry Gray Hood) was commissioned a first lieutenant in Company A on August 8. In addition to these residents, two other men in the Thirty-fifth were credited to the town: Alexander Webber, another heeler, on July 12,

Photograph, ca. 2006. Mortimer Johnson's family home is now 7 Harmony Court and carefully maintained by the current owners, especially the gracious prospect of the front gardens and lawn coming down to Nahant Road. Photographer: Bonnie Ayers D'Orlando. Nahant Historical Society.

14. "Soldier Bio" file, NHS.

15. Wilson, *Annals*, 103–4.

and George P. Stone, a Lynn coppersmith on July 29.[16] The Thirty-fifth Massachusetts would prove to be a hard luck outfit, at least for the men from Nahant, as all would be disabled or wounded. The Thirty-fifth went directly to the front and was assigned to the Ninth Corps under General Ambrose Burnside. It joined the Ninth Corps just after General John Pope's defeat at the Battle of Second Bull Run when George McClellan was attempting to restore order to the army. Elbridge Hood later related a story about this period. "I was lieutenant of pickets at Pope's retreat when General George B. McClellan ordered me to take 25 extra men and post them from Hunter's Chapel to Ball's Cross Roads, and while making the 'grand rounds' one of my men took me for a rebel and fired and dismounted me from my horse. The other pickets came for me and found that I was their officer. I forgave him for his carelessness and he became my best friend and is so . . . to the present day."[17]

The Thirty-fifth Massachusetts fought at South Mountain and then Antietam, the bloodiest single day of the war, where it lost 214 men, including 69 killed or mortally wounded. The Thirty-fifth belonged to the brigade that captured the famous Burnside Bridge. The new regiment was held in reserve at first, but late in the afternoon, they were placed in position along Otto's Lane. The eight hundred untried men of the Thirty-fifth withstood a strong rebel counterattack. Being green, they stayed in a situation where wiser, veteran soldiers would have employed the dictum that discretion is the better part of valor.[18] Lt. Elbridge Hood and George Stone were both wounded in this battle. Stone returned to the Thirty-fifth and was promoted to corporal, but he would be discharged for disability in August 1863. Hood was promoted to captain on December 15 (mustered January 19) but then discharged because of his wound.

Hood's stomach wound was serious. In his pension request after the war, he said the rebel bullet entered the "abdomen just above the naval [sic] and passing out back of the left hip, shattering the bone." Hood would experience "continued numbness and pain," and his

16. "Soldier Bio" file, NHS.

17. Lynn, MA GAR Hall, Member file Card for Elbridge G. Hood.

18. John Michael Priest, *Antietam: The Soldier's Battle* (New York, 1989), 285–300.

left leg would be "smaller than the right." He would be unable to "perform any bodily labor."[19] Despite the severity and damage, this was not enough to keep him from the service. After recuperating for a few months, he entered the Veteran Reserve Corps as a captain in December 1863.

The Veteran Reserve Corps (VRC) consisted of wounded or disabled men who could still do service. Formed into regiments, they generally performed garrison and guard duties to free healthy soldiers for combat.[20] Years later, Hood provided an excellent example of this work. "I had command of the guard that took General George P. Stuart and General Edward Johnston and 2,000 prisoners of war from the Battlefields of the Wilderness and Spotsylvania to Fort Delaware from Belle Plain, Virginia, May 13, 1864. General George P. Stuart sold his horse to a Yankee for $20 and used the money to give the rebel officers a breakfast on the transport boat, which was quite an elaborate affair for prisoners of war."[21] Probably owing to the severity of his wound, Hood's attempt to continue to serve his country failed, however, as his appointment was revoked in July 1864.

Photograph, USS *Maratanza*, ca. 1862–65. Charles Warren Johnson, a Nahant gardener, served on this 786-ton "double-ender" steam gunboat. See the windsails rigged for ventilation below decks. Courtesy of U.S. Naval Historical Center, Photo # NH 46629.

19. Elbridge G. Hood Pension Request, copy at Nahant Historical Society.

20. Lord, *They Fought for the Union*, 64.

21. Lynn, MA GAR Hall, Member file Card for Elbridge G. Hood.

Meanwhile, the Thirty-fifth fought at Fredericksburg and then was transferred west where it participated in the siege of Vicksburg and later in the pursuit of the rebels to Jackson, Mississippi. Alexander Webber, now a corporal, was wounded at Jackson and was eventually discharged or transferred to the Thirteenth Regiment VRC. He served with the VRC until November 1865. The other two heelers, Wheeler and Hanson, were discharged for disability, Wheeler in March 1863 and Hanson the following July. One other member of the Thirty-fifth Massachusetts also figures into our story. Charles T. Lawless enlisted in the Thirty-fifth in August 1862 and apparently was disabled and discharged. On August 22, 1864, he enlisted in the Thirteenth Regiment VRC, and this second enlistment was credited to Nahant. Like Webber, Lawless remained with the VRC until November 1865.[22]

Two soldiers, Marcellus Kidder and George Chesley Neal, who lived in Lynn but were credited to Nahant, joined the Thirty-third Massachusetts Volunteer Infantry. The Thirty-third was a large regiment, having twelve companies (two more than normal) and twelve hundred men when it left Massachusetts. Assigned to the Eleventh Corps, the Thirty-third fought at Chancellorsville and Gettysburg and then was transferred with the corps to the west, where it fought at Lookout Mountain and Missionary Ridge. The regiment then joined the Twentieth Corps and fought with William Tecumseh Sherman in the Atlanta campaign, including the battles of Resaca, Kennesaw Mountain, the March to the Sea, and the battle of Bentonville, North Carolina. Kidder enlisted on July 24, 1862. He would be promoted to corporal two years later and muster out with the regiment on July 11, 1865. Neal joined five days after Kidder. He was wounded at the Battle of Chancellorsville in May 1863 and later discharged for disability in March 1864. In August, he reenlisted in the Fourth Massachusetts Heavy Artillery, which was stationed in the defenses of Washington, D.C. Neal was promoted to first sergeant on April 1, 1865, and discharged with the regiment on June 17. Neal would enjoy a very full and productive life after the war, working as shoemaker, Lynn police detective, state policeman, member of the school committee, and president of the Lynn City Council.[23]

22. "Soldier Bio" file, NHS; *Mass. Soldiers*, 35th Mass. Vol. Inf.

23. "Soldier Bio" file, NHS; *Mass. Soldiers*, 33rd Mass. Vol. Inf.; Lynn *Daily Evening Item*, Dec. 14, 1929, Neal obituary.

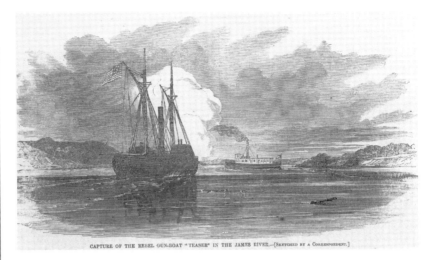

CAPTURE OF THE REBEL GUN-BOAT "TEASER" IN THE JAMES RIVER.—[SKETCHED BY A CORRESPONDENT.]

Previous page:
Photograph. Built
by Charles Warren
Johnson in 1851, this
Greek Revival house,
now 305 Nahant
Road, passed to his
brother, George L.
Johnson, whose
family is probably
shown in this image
about 1880. Nahant
Historical Society.

This page:
Line engraving.
USS *Maratanza*
(foreground)
captures CSS
Teaser in the James
River, Virginia,
July 4, 1862,
Harpers Weekly,
July–December
1862, possibly the
engagement where
Charles Warren
Johnson was mortally
wounded. Courtesy
of U.S. Naval
Historical Center,
Photo # NH 59216.

The other soldier who volunteered for three years that summer was Daniel L. Seavey. Seavey's enlistment in the Thirty-eighth Massachusetts Volunteer Infantry on August 22 was credited to Nahant. He apparently worked as a shoemaker in Lynn. Mustered into federal service that August, the Thirty-eighth initially went to Maryland and then to New Orleans with the Nineteenth Corps. The regiment participated in movements against Port Hudson and the Red River. In 1864, the Nineteenth Corps returned to Virginia and fought in the Shenandoah Valley, at Winchester, Fishers Hill, and Cedar Creek. In 1865, the Thirty-eighth went to Georgia and North Carolina at New Bern and Goldsboro (see next chapter). Seavey was discharged for disability in November 1863.[24]

Nahant also provided soldiers for the nine-month militia regiments called up by Lincoln in early August 1862. On August 20, James Campbell, a laborer from Ireland, enlisted in the Forty-third Massachusetts Militia. Known as the "Tiger Regiment," the Forty-third spent its nine months in North Carolina at New Bern, Goldsboro, and Washington. Mustered out in July 1863, Campbell joined the Fifty-sixth Massachusetts Volunteer Infantry that September. The Fifty-sixth was the first of the so-called "veteran regiments." The intention was to attract men, such as Campbell, who had already done service. The Fifty-sixth Massachusetts joined the Ninth Corps and saw hard fighting in Ulysses S. Grant's campaign against Robert E. Lee. The Massachusetts veterans fought in the

24. "Soldier Bio" file, NHS; *Mass. Soldiers*, 38th Mass. Vol. Inf. As we will see in chapter 5, two other men connected with postwar Nahant served with the 38th Mass.

Wilderness, Spotsylvania, North Anna, the Crater Fight at Petersburg, and the Weldon Railroad in 1864. They continued with siege operations around Petersburg into 1865 and participated in the general assault on the rebel lines on April 2, 1865. Campbell served with the regiment throughout that time and was promoted to sergeant. He mustered out with the regiment on July 12, 1865.[25]

Another Nahant resident who initially joined a nine-month regiment but continued on with further service was Arthur J. Bulfinch. Bulfinch enlisted in the Eleventh Battery, Massachusetts Light Artillery, on August 25, 1862. The Eleventh spent its nine months in northern Virginia in various garrisons. Mustered out in May 1863, the battery was reorganized the following fall as a three-year volunteer outfit, and Arthur Bulfinch reenlisted with his old outfit. The Eleventh Battery fought in the Wilderness in May 1864, Weldon Railroad, the siege of Petersburg, and at Fort Stedman, March 1865. Bulfinch mustered out of service with the battery on June 16, 1865.[26]

Charles Horton Palmer was a forty-three-year-old carpenter residing in Nahant, whose name had been on the town's 1853 militia list.

Palmer enlisted in the Eighth Massachusetts Militia on August 25, the same regiment as Alfred Tarbox. The Eighth Massachusetts was sent to New Bern, North Carolina. As mentioned earlier, the regiment saw no action because its companies were separated and widely distributed for guard and garrison duty. On its return to Washington, D.C., preparatory for mustering

Photograph, Frederic Tudor, merchant prince of Nahant and Boston and Civil War enlistment bounty funder, ca. 1850. Courtesy of Nahant Public Library.

25. "Soldier Bio" file, NHS; *Mass. Soldiers*, 43rd Mass. Vol. Inf., 56th Mass. Vol. Inf.

26. "Soldier Bio" file, NHS; *Mass. Soldiers*, 11th Mass. Battery.

out, the Eighth got caught up in the frenzy over Lee's invasion and the Battle of Gettysburg. The regiment was ordered to join the Army of the Potomac and participated in the pursuit of Lee back to Virginia. The Eighth returned to Massachusetts in early August and was mustered out on the seventh.[27]

On August 30, 1862, the town of Nahant held a meeting to "see what action the town would take" to raise the second quota issued for the nine-month men. The town voted to extend the $200 bounty voted on the previous March to any resident enlisting for nine months.[28] Whether it was this bounty or patriotism, a wave of enlistments swept the little peninsula in September 1862. However, if the bounty did convince many to enlist, we must be careful of our interpretation. Considering the attention that has been given to "bounty jumpers" during the Civil War, it is very easy to assign a purely mercenary motivation to anyone receiving a bounty. Using a considerable simplification, Civil War soldiers fell into four groups. The recruits of 1861 tended to enlist in the flush of patriotic fervor and in many cases had few responsibilities and ties at home. They tended to be younger men who had no families. The recruits of 1862, as mentioned earlier, had their patriotism tempered with the reality of the casualty lists. Patriotic they were, but they also completely understood the cost to their families. A private's pay of $13 a month did not go far, and if a soldier were killed, the financial future of his family could be in jeopardy (there was no life insurance). To many men torn between patriotism and responsibility, a $200 bounty allowed them to fulfill their wish to contribute to the war to preserve their country. It is the last two groups of soldiers, the draftees of 1863 and the bounty men of 1864, that provided the poor reputations. They either had to be forced into service or were offered increasingly larger bribes, which some took advantage of by collecting

Carte de visite, Elbridge Gerry Hood, ca. 1862. Courtesy of Nahant Public Library.

Above right: Field sword, ca. 1862. This sword is probably the one carried by Elbridge Gerry Hood at the Battle of Antietam. It has survived in battered condition since it was used not only as a toy by Hood family descendants but also painted blood red as a prop for mid-twentieth century amateur theatricals held in Nahant. Maker is unknown. Private collection.

27. "Soldier Bio" file, NHS; *Mass. Soldiers*, 8th Mass. Militia.

28. Wilson, *Annals*, 104.

the bounty, deserting, and then reenlisting in another regiment for another bounty, thus the term "bounty jumper." As stated, this is an oversimplification. There were patriotic men who joined after 1862 for bounty payments, including many three-year men who reenlisted in their regiments. The point is that we should not look down at the large number of Nahant residents who enlisted in nine-month regiments in September 1862, apparently after the town voted a $200 bounty. In many cases, they probably had family responsibilities, and the bounty, as well as the short-term service, enabled them to do their part; and nine-month regiments were sent in harm's way just like three-year volunteer units.

An interesting scene must have occurred on September 17, 1862, ironically, as we will see, on the day of the Battle of Antietam. Seven men from Nahant, six of them Johnsons, enlisted in the Forty-fifth Massachusetts Militia: Charles N. Babb, farmer; Edward J. Johnson, "Nahant fisherman"; Edwin W. Johnson, clerk; Hervey Shepard Johnson, "Nahant farmer"; Luther Scott Johnson; Sidney Coleman Johnson; Welcome Justin Johnson, "Nahant farmer."[29] Did they discuss this together? Did they plan to enter as one group? Did they travel to the recruiting station together? We will never know, but never before or after did so many leave Nahant for the war at the same moment. In addition, Edmund Buxton Johnson and Lorenzo P. Whitney enlisted in the Forty-fifth on September 26. All nine men served in Company F, and all remained with the regiment until it was mustered out on July 7, 1863. The Forty-fifth Massachusetts also went to New Bern,

Dress sword, engraved to the owner, Elbridge Gerry Hood, from the members of his company of the Thirty-fifth Massachusetts Volunteer Militia as a token of their esteem for his leadership. The Ames Company of Chicopee, Massachusetts, forged this sword of honor, also called a presentation sword. The sash also appears in Hood's carte de visite. Private collection.

---

29. Hervey Shepard and Welcome were brothers. According to a local legend, Hervey Shepard had a standing joke that he used. When someone said to him, "You're welcome," he would reply, "No, I'm Hervey Shepard."

Letter case used by Elbridge Gerry Hood, ca. 1860 or perhaps earlier, part of his civilian accessories used in wartime. Note the scored sun or starburst decoration. Nahant Historical Society.

North Carolina, and participated in the battles of Kinston and on the Goldsboro expedition. This service will be explored in the next chapter.[30]

The next recruit credited to Nahant in 1862 was John Simpson. According to the *Annual Town Report* of 1905, he was not a resident at the time of enlistment, simply credited to the town. Simpson had recently emigrated from Scotland and indicated he was a laborer. He joined the Twelfth Battery, Massachusetts Light Artillery, on December 3, 1862, and served with the battery in New Orleans until discharged because of disability on March 23, 1865. While Simpson was not a resident of the town at enlistment, he certainly became one after his military service and, as we will see, would become a constant reminder of the war for the people of Nahant and a tribute to their sense of duty and responsibility.[31] The last recruit credited to Nahant in 1862 also served in the Twelfth Battery.

---

30. "Soldier Bio" file, NHS; *Mass. Soldiers*, 45th Mass. Militia.

31. "Soldier Bio" file, NHS; *Mass. Soldiers*, 12th Battery, Mass. Lt. Art.

32. *Mass. Soldiers*, 12th Battery, Mass. Lt. Art; *Tenth Annual Report of the Town of Nahant for the Year ending February 28, 1863* (Lynn, MA, 1863), 7. Here, Austin Brewin and William Twiss got turned down the wrong path. It is not surprising since there were four William H. Perrys from Massachusetts who served, and two of them were from Lynn. And the story of these two is fascinating. According to his later obituary, William H. Perry "Jr." was thirteen when he left Lynn to collect his father's body, his father having been killed in the war. When he returned home, he enlisted on December 31, 1864. Brewin and Twiss believed this enlistment was credited to Nahant. The story is probably true. William H. Perry, 36-year-old shoemaker from Lynn, enlisted on July 5, 1861, in the 1st Mass. Heavy Artillery. He was wounded at Spotsylvania on May 19, 1864, and died on May 30. William H. Perry (no "Jr." attached), "18, heeler" from Lynn enlisted in December 1864. This fits the story well. His father enlisted in 1861, died in 1864, son retrieved body then enlists himself, lying about his age in the process. A wonderful tale, but having little to do with Nahant. The town records say a bounty was paid in the fiscal year running from March 1862 to February 1863 to "William H. Perry," and the only William H. Perry to enlist in that period was a seaman from Nantucket.

William H. Perry, an eighteen-year-old seaman from Nantucket, enlisted on December 4. He made corporal the following November and reached the rank of quartermaster sergeant by the time of his discharge on April 1, 1865.[32]

After 1862, Lincoln's government found recruiting far more difficult for several reasons. One problem concerned the depletion of the early three-year volunteer regiments. Unlike the South, who sent recruits into existing regiments, the North had followed the practice of raising new regiments for each request from the War Department. One reason for this was political. The governors of the various states appointed the field grade officers (all above the rank of captain) for volunteer regiments. Often this allowed political debts to be paid and political alliances to be cemented. Regiments already sent to the front had to rely on sending officers home to recruit, an inefficient system that took officers away from their regiments when they should have been

Color lithograph, ca. 1888, *Battle of Antietam*. During the bloodiest day of the war, September 17, 1862, Elbridge Gerry Hood and George P. Stone were injured in the vital struggle for Burnside Bridge. The Thirty-fifth Massachusetts suffered heavy casualties, with 212 killed or wounded. Kurz & Allison, Art Publishers, Chicago, Illinois. Courtesy of the Library of Congress.

training with them. As a result, many northern regiments were greatly reduced in numbers by the spring of 1863. On average, early northern regiments left home in 1861 and early 1862 with between eight hundred and one thousand men. By Gettysburg, those same regiments averaged two to three hundred, and some fought that battle with less than one hundred.

The draft would provide an answer. Congress passed the draft bill on March 3, 1863. All men drafted would receive the same pay and federal bounties as volunteers, but they would be sent to existing regiments. There were problems, including inadequate medical examinations (some regiments received draftees who were crippled or blind), and the act also allowed drafted men to hire a substitute or pay an exemption fee of $300. This became quite common, and the substitutes in particular came in for their share of abuse by the veterans they were sent among. In fact, whether from abuse, or bounty jumping, or a disinterest in the war itself, the percentage of deserters among draftees was very high.

The principal opposition to the draft came from urban and immigrant populations. Because of the high exemption fee, the draft turned the war into the "poor man's fight." Recent immigrants and foreigners found themselves caught in the draft without the means to pay the exemption. Hostility among the Irish, who had become disillusioned over the war, led to the famous New York City draft riots in July 1863, in which hundreds were killed. Yet the draft would be used until the end of the war to find replacements.[33]

Once again, Nahant reflects this national story. With so many men in the service already, Nahant provided only one name to the Union army in 1863, and he was a draftee who somehow became credited to Nahant. Otto Bush (or Busch) listed his residence as New York City and may have been a recent immigrant. He was drafted on August 21, 1863, and assigned to Company B, Ninth Massachusetts Volunteer Infantry. The "Fighting Ninth" was the first Irish regiment raised by Massachusetts. Their first colonel was Thomas Cass, whose statue now stands in Boston Common. Like all veteran regiments, the Ninth Massachusetts was pretty depleted when Bush joined them in the summer of 1863. The

---

33. Lord, *They Fought for the Union*, 6–7.

fact that Bush was German and was sent to an Irish regiment mattered little. The Ninth needed warm bodies, and Otto Bush was a warm body. The Ninth Massachusetts was in the Fifth Corps, Army of the Potomac, and became part of Grant's push against Lee in May 1864. Otto Bush was wounded at Spotsylvania. Soon after that, the original enlistment of the Ninth Massachusetts ran out, and the reenlisted men and draftees were transferred to the Thirty-second Massachusetts, which was in the same brigade as the Ninth. During his time with the Thirty-second, mostly involved in the siege of Petersburg, Bush managed to get promoted to corporal. However, on April 6, 1865, probably at Sailor's Creek, Bush was reported missing. Did he die or desert? And how did a German from New York City get credited to Nahant? We probably will never know.[34]

Eighteen sixty-four saw three men connected to Nahant go into the same unit, all for very short periods of time. On April 6, James Hogan, a laborer, enlisted in the Nineteenth Regiment, U.S. Infantry, and on April 20, he deserted. On May 6, both John Williams and Michael Mitchell enlisted in the same unit, the Nineteenth Infantry. Williams deserted five days later, and Mitchell "left the service" on May 19. Hogan was never heard from again, and neither was Williams. It seems that all three may have been simply credited to Nahant and not residents. After the war, Mitchell would become a resident and a respected businessman, so it appears his reasons for leaving the service were considered honorable. However, it is an interesting coincidence that all three entered a regular regiment at the same time and none lasted more than two weeks.[35]

Beyond the men detailed so far, there were five residents who apparently served in the war but their exact service is unknown. John Waters did enlist in the navy, but the exact dates have not been determined. Four other men are described as enlisting in "out-of-state" regiments. Hervey Hartwell Murdock's mother was of the Nahant Johnsons. He served in an out-of-state regiment but was credited to Nahant. Theodore M. Johnson, not related to the original Nahant Johnsons, also apparently served in an out-of-state regiment and did not return. George and Nelson Tarbox, brothers to Alfred, served out

34. "Soldier Bio" file, NHS; *Mass. Soldiers*, 9th Mass. Vol. Inf.

35. "Soldier Bio" file, NHS; *Mass. Soldiers*, 19th US Regulars.

of state, according to the best information. The three brothers did not remain in Nahant.[36]

Finally, Nahant being the unique community that it was, and still is, a few summer or part-time residents served in the war. Distinguishing if their connection to Nahant was prewar or postwar can be difficult, and their service is listed in other communities. But as Nahant has always accepted its summer residents with open arms, so should we accept their military service no matter where it occurred. Joseph Goode is simply listed as a "lieutenant who fought through the war." One suspects this service may have been naval since he became the captain of a trans-Atlantic steamer after the war. He also ran a lodging house and restaurant in Boston. His son owned W. P. Brush Co. of Nahant and Boston (now the Goode Brush Co.). Edward Crosby Johnson summered in Nahant and was related to the first Nahant Johnson. An 1860 graduate of Harvard, Johnson was commissioned as a first lieutenant in the Forty-fourth Massachusetts Militia on August 22, 1862. The nucleus of this nine-month regiment was the Fourth Massachusetts Militia. They served in the New Bern, North Carolina, campaign, participating in the Goldsboro expedition and the siege of Washington (see next chapter). After the war, he became an executive in a Boston department store.[37]

Charles Jackson Paine was a Boston lawyer and summer resident of Swallow Cave Road. Paine was commissioned a captain in the Twenty-second Massachusetts Volunteer Infantry on October 1, 1861. However, his service was short-lived, as he was discharged in January 1862, in order to accept a promotion to major in the Thirtieth Massachusetts. For some reason, the governor would not confirm this promotion, and Paine was mustered out on March 27. Paine gives the impression of a man who would not accept defeat, especially with his political connections.

It was probably those political connections that secured Paine the colonelcy of the Second Louisiana in October 1862. The name of this regiment might give pause, as many will assume he now commanded a rebel regiment. Actually, Paine became part of a little-known history

36. "Soldier Bio" file, NHS.

37. "Soldier Bio" file, NHS; *Mass. Soldiers*, 44th Mass. Militia.

of the Civil War. When New Orleans was captured in the spring of 1862, the military commander of the northern occupation forces was Benjamin F. Butler, a Democratic politician from Massachusetts. Butler found many in the area—Cajuns, Germans, Irish, northerners living in New Orleans, and "disaffected" southerners—who were willing to serve in blue uniforms. Butler enlisted these men in his own northern regiments and began to create new units. He organized twelve hundred volunteers as the First Regiment of Louisiana Volunteers. By September 1862, Butler reported that he had six hundred more to form a second regiment. Thus in October, Charles Jackson Paine was commissioned colonel of the Second Regiment of Louisiana Volunteers. Can we surmise that Paine was a Democrat? The governor of Massachusetts, John Albion Andrew, who had denied Paine his commission, was a Republican. Ben Butler was a Democrat and probably was familiar with such a prominent lawyer from Boston.[38]

Chas. J. Paine

Engraving, Charles Jackson Paine. This soldier and politician served first as a captain in the Twenty-second Massachusetts Volunteer Infantry and then later as a colonel of the Second Regiment of Louisiana Volunteers (Union). Artist: J. A. J. Wilcox. Courtesy of Nahant Public Library.

Although Butler was replaced at the end of 1862, Paine's luck would still hold. Butler's replacement was Nathaniel P. Banks, another Massachusetts politician, in fact a former governor. Discharged from the Second Louisiana in March 1864, Paine was promoted brigadier general on July 4, 1864, and brevetted to major general in January 1865.[39] Paine stayed in the service until August 15, 1866. After the war, he gained fame as a yachtsman, defending the America's Cup from 1870 to 1880.[40]

Summer resident Henry Wadsworth Longfellow's son, Charles Appleton—"Charley"—also enlisted in March 1863, at the age of eighteen. Charley had slipped away to war without telling his father,

38. "Soldier Bio" file, NHS; Richard Nelson Current, *Lincoln's Loyalists: Union Soldiers from the Confederacy* (New York, 1992), 89–93.

39. "Brevet" means temporary rank.

40. "Soldier Bio" file, NHS.

who thought his son "altogether too young to go into the army."[41] He apparently tried to join the regular army, but a missing left thumb (a childhood accident with a shotgun) prevented that. He showed

Carte de visite, Charles Appleton Longfellow, ca. 1862, in his uniform as a second lieutenant in the First Massachusetts Cavalry. Officers were expected to provide their own uniform, kit, and horses. His father, poet Henry Wadsworth Longfellow, outfitted "Charley." Photographer: J. W. Black, Boston. Courtesy of National Park Service Longfellow National Historic Site.

up at the camp of Battery A, First Massachusetts Artillery, because he knew the captain, W. H. McCartney. McCartney wrote Charley's father of his presence and suggested he fool the boy into thinking he had enlisted until the father's wishes could be known. Longfellow resigned himself to the inevitable and wrote to McCartney to let Charley really enlist, and then the poet pulled all the strings he could to get Charley an officer's commission.[42]

Charley soon received a commission as a second lieutenant in the First Massachusetts Cavalry. Officers were expected to provide their own uniform, kit, and horses, so Longfellow proceeded to outfit his son at a cost of $779.75.[43] Within two weeks, Charley was named acting adjutant. To his great disappointment, his regiment missed the Battle of Chancellorsville that May 1862. Then, Charley came down with "camp fever." Longfellow went to Washington to administer to his son, and, despite the advice of some doctors, he believed Charley's best chance for recovery would be among the cool, ocean breezes of Nahant. By the end of June, they were at the family's cottage in Nahant where Charley enjoyed a pleasant, if over-long convalescence. A letter threatening to charge him with being "AWOL" arrived (even the Longfellows had to follow the rules), and Charley returned to his regiment.[44]

When Charley left Nahant in August 1863, his father procured him another officer's kit costing $616.48.[45] The First Massachusetts Cavalry spent the late summer and early fall of 1863 chasing John

Mosby's guerrilla raiders, foraging for food, and scouting for the enemy. In December, the regiment participated in the Mine Run campaign. During one action near New Hope Church, Charley was struck by a minie ball that passed under his shoulder blade, nicked his spine, and passed out the other side. Although gravely wounded, with the prospect of paralysis, Charley was actually lucky he was alive. Had the ball wavered a fraction of an inch in either direction, it would have killed him.[46] Longfellow came to Washington and brought his son home to Cambridge. Although he expected to recover and rejoin his regiment, Charley received word in February 1864 that he had been given a disability discharge. Disappointed at the end of his military career, Charley sailed for Europe the following November. Although he would live an active life, he died in 1893 at the relatively young age of forty-nine of a paralysis that probably resulted from his old war wound.[47]

41. "Charley Longfellow Goes to War," *Harvard Library Bulletin*, Spring 1960, 60.

42. "Charley Longfellow Goes to War," *Harvard Library Bulletin*, Spring 1960, 61–68.

43. "Charley Longfellow Goes to War," *Harvard Library Bulletin*, Spring 1960, 73.

44. "Charley Longfellow Goes to War," *Harvard Library Bulletin*, Spring 1960, 80–81.

45. "Charley Longfellow Goes to War," *Harvard Library Bulletin*, Winter 1960, 283.

46. "Charley Longfellow Goes to War," *Harvard Library Bulletin*, Winter 1960, 292.

47. "Charley Longfellow Goes to War," *Harvard Library Bulletin*, Winter 1960, 294–303.

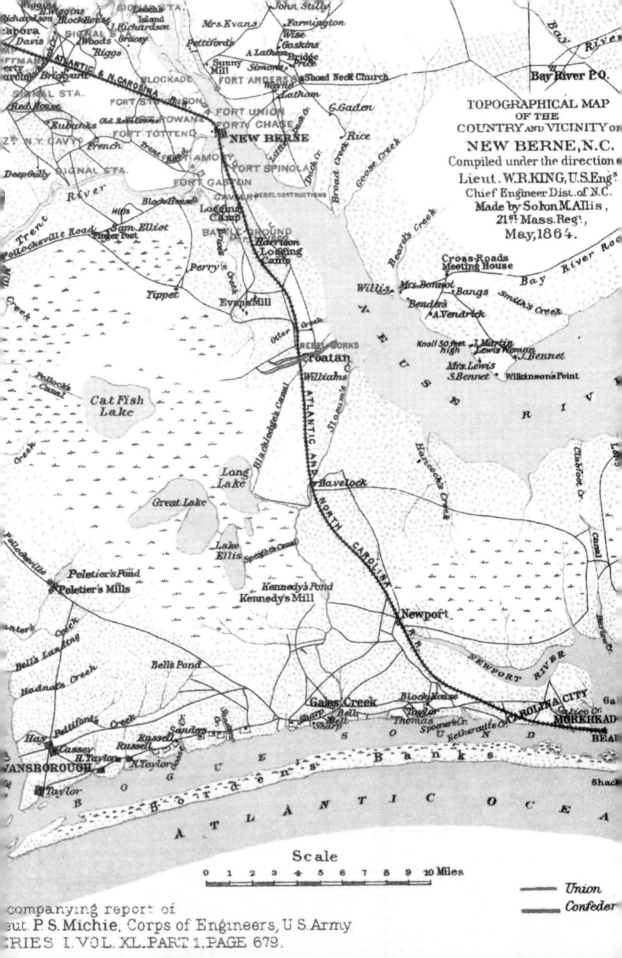

TOPOGRAPHICAL MAP OF THE COUNTRY AND VICINITY OF NEW BERNE, N.C. Compiled under the direction of Lieut. W.R. KING, U.S. Engs Chief Engineer Dist. of N.C. Made by Solon M. Allis, 21st Mass. Regt, May, 1864.

Scale
0 1 2 3 4 5 6 7 8 9 10 Miles

—— Union
—— Confeder

companying report of
eut. P.S. Michie, Corps of Engineers, U.S. Army
RIES I. VOL. XL. PART 1. PAGE 679.

three

NEW BERN, NORTH CAROLINA

IT BECOMES QUITE EVIDENT IN STUDYING THE STORY OF THE SOLDIERS from
Nahant that two things, a time period and a place, concentrated much
of their war experience. The town experienced its greatest losses, both
in men leaving the town and on the battlefield, in the three months
of July to September 1862. Of the thirty residents who served in the
war, fifteen enlisted in that three-month period. Six of the eleven men
credited to Nahant also left at that time, and of the twenty-seven other
men connected to the town as postwar residents, burials, and others,
twelve began their Civil War experience in those three months as
well. Not only did men leave the town in large numbers, but also all
the Nahant residents injured in the war were wounded or died in that
three-month period. Charles Warren Johnson, serving in the navy,
died on July 20. George F. Newhall was killed at the Battle of Second
Bull Run, August 29. Three days later, on September 1, Patrick Riley
was wounded at the Battle of Chantilly and died of his wounds that
December. On September 17, at the Battle of Antietam, town residents
Elbridge Gerry Hood and William L. Rand as well as George P. Stone,
a man credited to Nahant, were wounded.[1] Indeed, if you add to this
the fact that Charles Babb and six of the Johnsons all enlisted in the
Forty-fifth Massachusetts on September 17, it stands out as probably
the darkest day of the whole war for the little town.

In addition to this time frame, the other collective experience for
the men of Nahant involved New Bern, North Carolina. Nahant

Map of the Country
and Vicinity of
New Berne, N.C.,
compiled under the
direction of Lieut.
W. R. King, U.S.
Engrs. Made by
Solon M. Allis,
Twenty-first
Massachusetts
Regiment, May
1864. Julius Bien &
Co. Lithographers,
NY. *Atlas of the
Official Records
of the Civil War.*

men fought at all the famous battles, at Second Bull Run, Antietam, Fredericksburg, Chancellorsville, Gettysburg, Vicksburg, Wilderness, Spotsylvania, Petersburg, and Sherman's march through Georgia, but no action provided such common ground as the now almost forgotten campaign around New Bern. No fewer than twenty of the men connected to Nahant served at New Bern at some time during the war. However, the real significance comes from the enlistment of the Johnsons in the Forty-fifth Massachusetts. They were the town of Nahant, and what they experienced, reinforced by veterans who later moved to the town, was what the town remembered. New Bern may have been a secondary, backwater campaign scarcely recognized today, but to Nahant, it was very important.[2]

The New Bern campaign initially grew out of the naval blockade of the South. When the war broke out, General Winfield Scott, Commander of the Army in early 1861, proposed a strategy that became known as the "Anaconda Plan." Like a giant snake, the federal government should impose a naval blockade, gain control of the Mississippi River to cut the South in two, and simply hold on until the South strangled. Although the North lacked the patience to simply wait, the essential elements of Scott's plan were employed. The North did not have an adequate number of ships available in 1861 to patrol every inlet and cove, and so the navy took advantage of every geographic feature it could. The long shoals and reefs along Cape Hatteras in North Carolina provided ample hiding places for rebel ships. Rather than commit vessels it did not have to patrol the outside, the Navy knew that controlling the area *inside* the reefs would be far easier and more efficient. In August, a combined naval and land force, the latter commanded by Benjamin Butler of Massachusetts, attacked and captured Beaufort.[3]

---

1. Rand would later be wounded at Fredericksburg and be killed in battle in March 1865.

2. Specific information on the New Bern operation, particularly in 1862–63, had to be ferreted out of widely diverse sources.

3. E. B. Long, *The Civil War Day by Day: An Almanac, 1861–1865* (Garden City, NY, 1971), 122; Shelby Foote, *The Civil War, A Narrative: Fort Sumter to Perryville* (New York, 1958), 352.

The naval problem settled, the War Department now saw an opportunity to cut the Weldon Railroad. The Weldon Railroad was the lifeline of Richmond to the Deep South, bringing supplies from Florida, Georgia, and the Carolinas up to the Confederate capital and the Army of Northern Virginia. The line ran south from Petersburg, Virginia, to Weldon, North Carolina, through Goldsboro and Wilmington, then into South Carolina. In early 1862, Northern forces, now under the command of Ambrose Burnside, began to push out from Beaufort northwest toward New Bern. Burnside captured New Bern on March 14. Situated almost due east of Goldsboro, New Bern would become the center of all operations against the Weldon Railroad. However, this always remained a secondary operation for the War Department, and the commanders there were never given adequate forces to push the rebel defenders out of Goldsboro.[4]

The secondary nature of this operation can be seen in the fall of 1862. As discussed in the previous chapter, that summer Lincoln called for three hundred thousand three-year volunteers and three hundred thousand militia for nine months. Of the Massachusetts units connected to Nahant, the three-year regiments were assigned to the Army of the Potomac or in the Mississippi campaigns, while the nine-month militia units were sent to New Bern. Thus, the men from Nahant who went into the Thirty-fifth Massachusetts, such as William Hanson and Elbridge Hood, fought at Antietam, while the Fifth, Eighth, Forty-third, Forty-fourth, and Forty-fifth Massachusetts militia regiments went to New Bern. Essentially, the commander, now Major General John G. Foster, was told he had nine months to complete the operation. As soon as the militia units arrived and could be organized, Foster began his march to Goldsboro.

Foster's army left New Bern on December 11. Three days later, they fought a sharp battle and captured the town of Kinston, roughly halfway between New Bern and Goldsboro. Engagements followed the next three days: at White Hall, Goshen's Swamp, and, on December 17, near Goldsboro itself. However, Foster could not capture the railroad

---

4. Long, *The Civil War Day by Day*, 184.

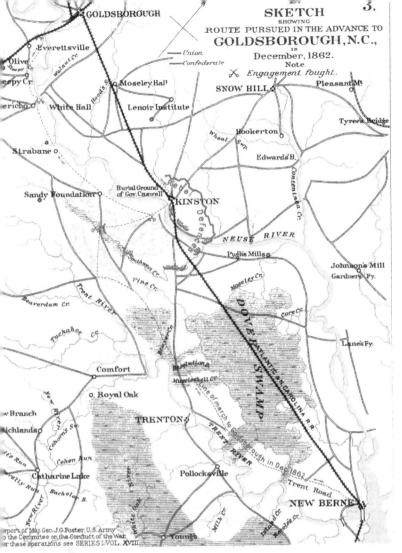

Map: Sketch of
Route Pursued in
the Advance to
Goldsborough, N.C.,
ca. December 1862,
from the report of
Major General J. G.
Foster. Julius Bien &
Co. Lithographers,
NY. *Atlas of the
Official Records
of the Civil War.*

junction, and he marched his tired men back to New Bern. In January, Foster made another reconnaissance toward Goldsboro but did not have the forces to take the town. Then the military situation changed dramatically.[5]

Taking advantage of the lull in the fighting in Northern Virginia, Robert E. Lee sent General James Longstreet and two divisions of his corps south of Richmond. Longstreet was assigned to command the Department of Virginia and North Carolina. The forces in North Carolina consisted of seventy-five hundred men at Wilmington under Brigadier General Chase Whiting and eleven thousand at Goldsboro under Longstreet's friend, Major General Daniel Harvey Hill. Longstreet's responsibilities were twofold: first (and foremost according to President Jefferson Davis), protect Richmond from the south; second, gather supplies (forage, grain, foodstuffs) from the rich farmland of southeast Virginia and North Carolina for the Army of Northern Virginia.

Longstreet ordered Whiting to send half his force north to Hill for use in foraging; then he went to Goldsboro in early March to confer with Hill. They both decided that an attempt should be made to recapture New Bern. In addition to the troops being sent by Whiting, Longstreet

5. Long, *The Civil War Day by Day*, 295–312.

agreed to send Hill one of his brigades from Richmond. However, when Hill arrived at New Bern on March 8, he was outnumbered by the Yankee defenders. Whiting never sent the soldiers, and the brigade from Richmond was late. Hill could only demonstrate outside the town and gather the precious supplies in the area.

Longstreet next ordered Hill to attack the town of Washington, almost directly north of New Bern. Reinforced this time, Hill laid siege to Washington on March 30. Although he greatly outnumbered the garrison, he did not feel it prudent to order a direct assault. For two weeks he besieged the town and gathered the supplies in the area. Foster withdrew into his defenses at first, fearing rebel attacks elsewhere, and left Hill alone. Finally Foster sent a relief force, but it was the navy that broke the siege, running its ships past rebel batteries. Hill, having gathered everything in the area that was not nailed down, pulled back to Goldsboro.

Foster made a tentative advance toward Kinston between April 27 and May 1, fighting a few small engagements along the way. In early May, General Joseph Hooker, new commander of the Army of the Potomac, moved against the Army of Northern Virginia, and Lee ordered Longstreet and his divisions to rejoin him.[6] For the South, the situation in North Carolina stabilized to where it had always been, and, without the presence of Longstreet's divisions, D. H. Hill was thrown back on the defensive. Foster's time was also running out, as his nine-month militia regiments would be going home in June. He made another advance in late May, fighting once again at Kinston and at Gum Swamp, but in the end pulled back.[7]

The New Bern-Goldsboro theater would continue to take a back seat until the end of the war. Federal forces raided out of New Bern in October and December 1863 and January 1864. On February 1 and 2,

6. They would not be in time, and Lee would have to fight the Battle of Chancellorsville without them.

7. Jeffry D. Wert, *General James Longstreet: The Confederacy's Most Controversial Soldier—A Biography* (New York, 1993), 228–38; Long, *The Civil War Day by Day*, 327, 338, 355.

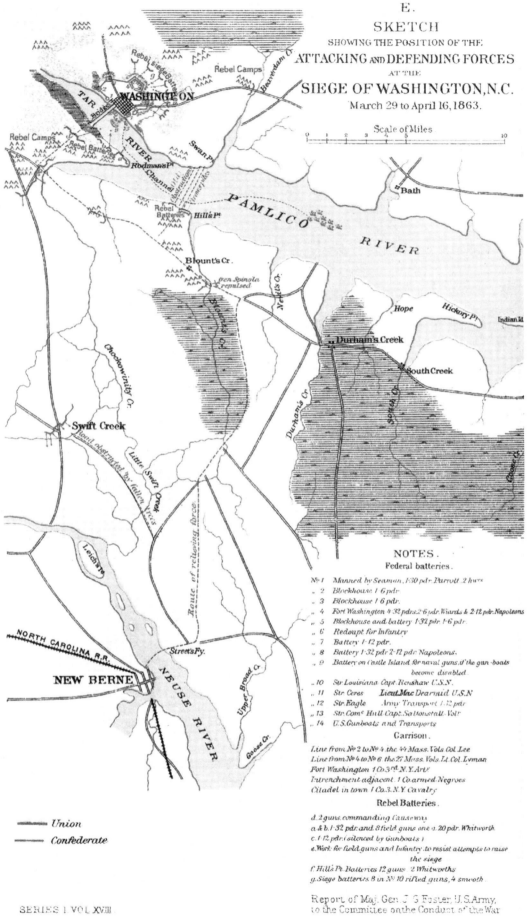

rebel forces under General George Pickett attacked New Bern and were repulsed. Another rebel attack failed in May. The area would become a focus only when William Tecumseh Sherman marched north in 1865. On February 22, 1865, Sherman's army captured Wilmington, but by March 7, Sherman realized that New Bern would make a better supply depot and so shifted General John Schofield's forces there. While Sherman marched north, Schofield would push west, and the two would meet at Goldsboro.

As Schofield marched west, rebel forces attacked him as he neared Kinston, and a second Battle of Kinston occurred on March 8–10. Schofield resumed his advance and captured Kinston on March 14. From there he advanced toward Goldsboro. Meanwhile, Sherman was pushing north against Confederate General Joe Johnston's army. Johnston struck at Sherman at Bentonville, just southeast of Goldsboro, on March 19. The resulting three-day battle was the last major engagement between these foes. Inevitably, Johnston's greatly outnumbered forces had to withdraw, and on March 22, Sherman and Schofield met at Goldsboro, the rebel town finally in Northern hands.[8]

As indicated earlier, Nahant's presence at New Bern was particularly strong. The Fifth, Forty-third, Forty-fourth, and Forty-fifth Massachusetts Militia and the Twenty-fourth Massachusetts Volunteer Infantry all participated in the advance on Goldsboro in December 1862, which included the Battle of Kinston and White Hall, as well as the operations in the spring of 1863. The Forty-fourth Massachusetts was besieged at Washington, and the Fifth Massachusetts was part of the force sent to relieve the siege. The Fifth also participated in the Gum Swamp expedition in late May. In the Fifth Massachusetts were two men who became residents of Nahant after the war, William Gibbs and William Hildreth,[9] and one who found an eternal home in Nahant. Edwin F. Whitney was born in Charlestown, Massachusetts, and enlisted from there but was related to the Whitney family of Nahant. Edwin died at Academy Green Hospital in New Bern on

Map: Sketch Showing the Position of the Attacking and Defending Forces at the Siege of Washington, N.C., March 29 to April 16, 1863. Julius Bien & Co. Lithographers, NY. *Atlas of the Official Records of the Civil War.*

8. Long, *The Civil War Day by Day*, 460, 493, 547, 642–56.

9. Chapter 5 details all the veterans who moved to the town after the war.

February 3, 1863, apparently of disease. However, he was buried in Nahant in the Whitney family plot rather than at Charlestown.[10]

William J. Johnson served in the Twenty-fourth Massachusetts, a three-year volunteer regiment that spent its service on the coast. The regiment participated in the capture of New Bern on March 14, 1862, and in the operations against Goldsboro in December before being transferred to the force attempting to capture Charleston. James Campbell served with the Forty-third Massachusetts throughout the action between December 1862 and June 1863. Summer resident First Lieutenant Edward C. Johnson served with the Forty-fourth Massachusetts, which participated in the Goldsboro expedition in December, losing eight killed and ten wounded at White Hall on the sixteenth, and as mentioned, was at Washington during the siege in April 1863.

Also in the area was the Eighth Massachusetts Militia. Charles H. Palmer, Alfred Tarbox, and a postwar resident of Nahant, John Trefry, served in this unit, although they saw no real action. The companies of the Eighth Massachusetts were detached and scattered in various guard duties. This was similar to the Second Massachusetts Heavy Artillery, which arrived in New Bern in the summer of 1863 as replacement for the nine-month regiments that had departed in June. Heavy Artillery regiments tended to be very large and, despite their name, usually employed as infantry. Like the Eighth, the companies of the Second Heavies were broken up and scattered in various posts. Among their numbers was Dwight Lamphear, who would become a resident of Nahant after the war.

Another postwar resident who also served at New Bern was Frank Deshon of the Thirty-eighth Massachusetts Volunteer Infantry. Deshon enlisted on August 20, 1862, into this well-traveled regiment, as described in the previous chapter. Other members of the Thirty-eighth connected to Nahant were Daniel L. Seavey, credited to the town on enlistment, and Charles Quimby, also destined to be a postwar resident. Both Quimby and Seavey had left the regiment by 1865, but

10. "Soldier Bio" file, NHS.

Deshon remained. The Thirty-eighth Massachusetts formed part of Schofield's force that left New Bern and advanced west on Goldsboro, fighting at Kinston along the way. At the same time, the Thirty-third Massachusetts, with Marcellus Kidder and postwar resident Fred A. Trefethan, marched with Sherman southwest of Goldsboro and fought in the Battle of Bentonville.[11]

However, there is no doubt that the greatest connection between Nahant and New Bern came from the Forty-fifth Massachusetts Militia, particularly Company F, which contained Charles Babb, Edmund Johnson, Edward Johnson, Edwin Johnson, Hervey Shepard Johnson, Luther Johnson, Sidney Johnson, Welcome Johnson, and Lorenzo Whitney. These men would provide Nahant's most vibrant association with the Civil War because they would function as the backbone of the community by serving as elected and appointed officials after the war. It is they who left us with the most vivid images of the New Bern campaign.

The Forty-fifth Massachusetts, called the "Cadet Regiment" because over forty of its commissioned officers were members of the "Boston Cadets," a prewar militia company known for its drill, was mustered into service on September 26, 1862. They embarked on ships, arriving at Beaufort, North Carolina, on November 5. From there, they boarded a train for New Bern. As part of Foster's expedition to

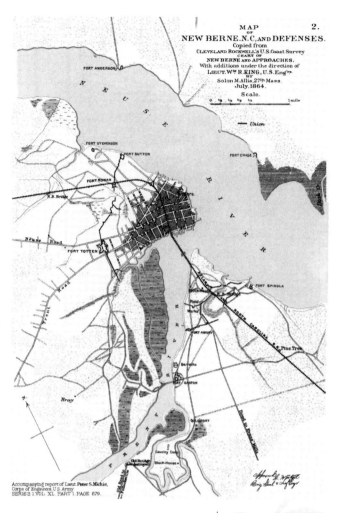

MAP 2.

NEW BERNE. N.C. AND DEFENSES.
Copied from
CLEVELAND ROCKWELL'S U.S. Coast Survey
CHART OF
NEW BERNE AND APPROACHES.
With additions under the direction of
LIEUT. W.m R. KING, U.S. Eng.rs
BY
Solon M. Allis, 27th Mass
July, 1864.
Scale.

Accompanying report of Lieut. Peter S. Michie,
Corps of Engineers, U.S. Army
SERIES 1 VOL. XL PART 1 PAGE 679.

Map of New Berne. N.C., and Defenses, copied from Cleveland Rockwell's U.S. Coast Survey. Chart of New Berne and Approaches, with additions under the direction of Lieut. Wm. R. King, U.S. Engrs. by Solon M. Allis, Twenty-seventh Massachusetts, July 1864. Julius Bien & Co. Lithographers, NY. *Atlas of the Official Records of the Civil War*

---

11. Information on these soldiers and units comes from the "Soldier's Biographies" file at the Nahant Historical Society and *Mass. Soldiers.* See also chapters 2 and 5 for more information.

Goldsboro in December, the Forty-fifth first saw action at the Battle of Kinston. This action cost the Forty-fifth Massachusetts fifteen killed and forty-three wounded.[12] A typed copy of a newspaper clipping exists in the Nahant Historical Society that reproduces a letter sent by one of the Nahant men in Company F. The letter describes his experience in this battle.

Camp Amory 45 Reg., Co. F., Newbern

Dear Reporter: I will try to give you some account of the battle of Kinston.

Thursday, Dec. 10, found us at daybreak in line before our camp, ready for a move. Soon the order came "Right face—forward—march!" and our regiment moved on towards Newbern, to join the others on that long march to Goldsboro. I will not attempt any account of the march, only as regards myself, and mine was the experience of many others. Our progress was very slow the first part of the day, getting the several brigades and the long baggage trains in order to move. About two o'clock we got to moving in right earnest. The load on my back grew heavy and heavier. I began to think I was in a "tight corner" with only one "look" and that was to keep up. Just before dark, however, I had a streak of luck—for over the fence, just at my side, a negro boy came, all out of breath, running away from his master. "Hello, Tom!" said I, "where are you going?" "I'll go with you, massa, if you'll let me." Tom was as glad to take my load and follow me as I was to be relieved of it.

About eight we reached the place where we were to bivouac for the night. Other regiments, that had preceded us, had their campfires already burning—and what a sight! Thousands of fires burning, filling the air with smoke and illuminating acres of ground where our little army was encamped—a sight familiar only to the soldier.

12. *Mass. Soldiers*, 45th Mass. Militia; Albert W. Mann, *History of the Forty-fifth Regiment Massachusetts Volunteer Militia, "The Cadet Regiment"* (Boston, 1908).

But he has no time to admire, even if he had a wish to. Too tired
from his day's march, his scanty meal must be eaten. I shared
with Tom, cooked my coffee, spread my blanket, and slept. Up
before light next morning, and on our march—Tom with two
more blankets on his back, mine making three.
The rebels had felled large trees across the road,
[which] caused a good many delays. About
noon I saw the first dead rebel, lying by the
roadside—killed by our advancing cavalry. A
little farther on lay a dead horse, and near him
a dying rebel. This began to look like careless
business. We halted, ate our dinners and carefully
. . . expecting an attack.

Nine o'clock found us again by our campfires,
glad to lie down anywhere. The next morning
the boys confiscated all the pigs they could find. I
know we had plenty of pork for breakfast. I met
Tom with a whole hog's head. At ten (forenoon)
on moved the column again. Eleven, and our
battery guns told us something surely was ahead.
The infantry opened on the right and left to let
the artillery pass through. Battery after battery
dashed past us. We formed in line of battle and were ordered to
rest. The firing ahead having ceased, we were glad to lie down on
the grass, and two-thirds of the men were asleep in a short time.
We were very tired, and the sun shining warm upon us, we had a
good nap. No more firing being heard, we prepared for the night.
Now a rush for the Virginia rail fences, each company securing
a pile for the night fires. Some out foraging after potatoes and
everything they could lay their hands on; and poor piggy came in,
in wholes and halves; each soldier was cooking on his own hook,
and in every conceivable way. Every house was ransacked from
cellar to attic by some of the boys for "relics." Not much sleep
tonight—too much cooking, and fixing, and fretting. None seemed
to think of the morrow—the present was enough—and in that

Carte de visite,
Edward J. Johnson
in civilian dress,
ca. 1866. Courtesy
of Nahant Public
Library.

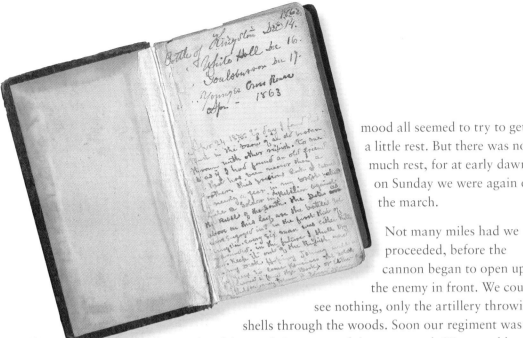

During the war, Edward J. Johnson carried this King James Version Bible, printed and published in Edinburgh by J. A. Ballantyne, 1857. Here, he recorded information about the New Bern campaign. Nahant Historical Society.

mood all seemed to try to get a little rest. But there was not much rest, for at early dawn on Sunday we were again on the march.

Not many miles had we proceeded, before the cannon began to open upon the enemy in front. We could see nothing, only the artillery throwing shells through the woods. Soon our regiment was ordered forward. I was one of the rear guard. We passed by the battery, along a narrow cart road, which led into the woods. This wood proved to be a swamp, with mud up to our knees. Just then a shell from our guns passed close over my head, at which I suddenly settled deeper into the mud. Another, from the rebels, caused a second dodge; but "forward" was the word, and we pushed ahead, while the shells from each side began to whistle over our heads in good earnest. Still we pushed on to the edge of the wood, amid a perfect shower of bullets. Here we were ordered to lie down and shelter ourselves as best we could, firing our guns at will—the rebels all the while pouring a leaden hail upon us, of shot, grape and cannister [sic]. I cannot describe it. The balls whistled by us in every direction.

I was on the extreme left, and worked my way through that terrible fire to join my company on the right. But it was hard to see our men lying dead in that swamp—one man, from Company B, close beside me. I helped one poor wounded man from the swamp, then rallied around our colors, and passed out of the woods. I saw no wounded rebels on the field—they had carried them all off.

You will think this a brief account of the battle, but its scenes are yet too fresh in my memory, and they are so full of horror. I do not want to enlarge upon them, or recall the events of a day like Sunday, Dec. 14, 1862. The rebels gave way after holding us about three hours. We took a good many prisoners. I saw them brought in by squads of fifty and seventy-five. They were ragged and dirty, but, if clothed and washed up, would have made good-looking men. How glad we were, after the battle, to meet one another, till all the Nahant boys were reported safe.

At dusk we halted near the town, on a plain, building our fires of wood from somebody's lumberyard. I lay down exhausted, not to move till I was obliged to. Now began to come in the plunder—quilts, sheets, sugar, pots, kettles, in fact anything the boys could get. I could not share in any of this sport but contented myself with lying on the ground and seeing the rest. It was laughable to see Tom trying on a nice white shirt. I asked him if he had found him a coat. "Oh, yes, massa," says Tom, "heaps of um!"—and the last I saw of him he was disappearing through the smoke, well fitted to a new suit (his freedom suit, literally) and with a good bundle under his arm. At Kinston I saw the stocks in front of the jail—and they are queer-looking things for human limbs to be fastened in. I thought, as we examined them, that they would be a strange sight in New England. You would have laughed to see the negroes—squad after squad, great and small—laying all the baggage they could carry off on their heads and backs, and going on their way rejoicing with us towards Newbern. Some carried their little ones in their arms. One family I saw keeping up with the trains day after day, "toting" along two or three of their children. In the streets at Kinston I saw a little negro boy marching gravely along with a general's hat on, and a sword by his side!

Although the letter doesn't mention it, the Forty-fifth was slightly engaged at White Hall on the sixteenth, suffering four killed and sixteen wounded.

From January 26 to April 25, the Forty-fifth Massachusetts got to know New Bern very well, for they served as Provost Guard. The Provost Guard was the Civil War equivalent of the modern MP or Military Police. They protected army stores and

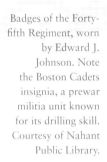

Badges of the Forty-fifth Regiment, worn by Edward J. Johnson. Note the Boston Cadets insignia, a prewar militia unit known for its drilling skill. Courtesy of Nahant Public Library.

buildings placed off limits (called "Safeguards"), quelled disturbances, and guarded prisoners, both the enemy and their own men who had broken army rules. Obviously, they were present during D. H. Hill's thrust at New Bern in March. The Forty-fifth participated in Foster's probe, April 27 to May 1. They captured a rebel earthwork on April 28, losing one killed and four wounded. Welcome Johnson later wrote a reminiscence of this movement for the unit's history.

ON THE SKIRMISH LINE AT DOVER CROSS ROADS

April 27th, 1863—Upon our arrival at Batchelder's Creek, our outer picket station, we found on the railroad track a monitor car, plated with iron, carrying two howitzers. It was manned by an officer and detail from our regiment, and placed in front of the engine.

It will be remembered that Company B, Captain Churchill, and Company F, Captain Daland, were on the skirmish line that day, marching ten to twenty rods in advance of the column. These two companies took turns in leading, the company whose turn it was to lead, sending out eight or ten men, deployed on either side of the road to guard against surprise. I very distinctly remember marching ahead of the savage-looking monitor car. We marched in the advance several miles that day, when the regiment halted and went into bivouac for the night. The two companies were ordered ahead as advanced picket guard, marching about two miles when we came to a camp, built of rails and covered with pine boughs, which the rebels had just left. This we made our headquarters, and pickets were sent out from there. I remember being posted about twenty rods from this camp, with my brother, H. S. Johnson. When it came his turn to lie down and take a nap, there came one of those southern showers. The rain worked under his rubber blanket, and he soon lay in a puddle of water.

While standing guard, I heard the limbs and dry boughs crack and break in the darkness but couldn't tell whether the noise was made by men, pigs, or possum, but it was surely caused by something. At noon next day, the Forty-Fifth was reinforced by the Forty-Third Massachusetts, and General Palmer had arrived with his command.

The column having come up, our two companies were again sent in the advance about fifteen to twenty rods, to guard against sudden attack, and soon came to a place where the rails had been entirely removed.

We passed several rebel picket posts, the enemy were gradually falling back—Company B, having led the advance for some time, was fatigued and was relieved by Company F. We passed another picket post and came to a plantation of about forty acres, where was a house, corncribs and a shed.

Rebel cavalry had been seen crossing the railroad track and going into the woods on our left. The column came to a halt, Colonel Codman acting as Brigadier-General, and Major Sturgis, with field glasses, came to the front to view the situation. Five men were seen to leave the house and walk obliquely towards the woods, on the left of the railroad. Captain Daland was ordered to send two files of men in pursuit and detailed my brother H. S. Johnson, Frank Howe, James Chick and myself. We were in the extreme advance.

We had a long hard run after those men, part of it over ploughed ground, but gained on the rebels for such they proved to be. My brother ordered them to halt, which they refused to do. He then brought his gun to his shoulder, with "Halt, or I fire." This brought them to a stand. The writer being quick on his feet, ran on ahead about eight or ten rods, and captured the men. They said, "We haven't done anything." I replied, "If you haven't we won't harm you, but we want you to come with us." This ended the conversation.

As we passed the house referred to, my brother and I stopped to glance within. As we opened the door of an outside building we spied on a shelf near the door, "a stew and Indian dumplings."

My brother had just grabbed a dumpling when we heard firing from the rebel earthworks across the track. We waited for no more "dumplings," but hurried our prisoners to Colonel Codman, and then rejoined the "skirmish line."

Reinforced by Company E, on our left, we charged over nearly the same route where we had taken our prisoners, into a concealed earthwork, which was walled up as evenly as a cellar wall. Inside at the left corner stood a wounded rebel, he couldn't step. Our colors were honored by many cheers, which were replied to by the rebel yell in the woods not far away! The roll was called inside the work, and then we started out to find the missing ones. One man, H. M. Putney of Company F, was found dead near the rail fence. Corporal Richards of E was wounded. The rebels could easily have killed, or made prisoners of, our entire little squad, for when we were pursuing the two men, we passed directly under the guns of the garrisoned earthwork. Comrade L. P. Whitney of our company said he counted twelve rebel pickets run up the track, after we had passed the corncribs, and thought it was all up for us. After a while the house was examined and a place in the wall was found that could be taken down, in which was a record, showing that these men had been paid half a dozen times for shooting our pickets, receiving five or six dollars for each man killed. There is no doubt but that one of these men was a most desperate character. It was said that these men were afterwards taken into the woods, tried and shot. I hope it was not so. The earthwork having been taken and the enemy dispersed,

Carte de visite, Sidney Coleman Johnson, ca. October 1862, photographed soon after enlistment in his uniform of the Forty-fifth Massachusetts Volunteer Militia. Courtesy of Nahant Public Library.

we started back over the same route over which we had advanced, arriving at our old camp, after a long march, very much fatigued. None who participated in that march will ever forget it.

On April 30th, while in this camp, we received a large kettle of baked beans, sent up by the Invalid Squad, left at Camp Massachusetts—and just at that time those beans were thoroughly appreciated. On our return to Camp Massachusetts the thought came to us, it mattered not how humble our position, we were in the service of our country, engaged in the greatest conflict between right and wrong the Western Hemisphere had ever experienced. I call to mind that when we fell into line the morning of April 27th, to go on the expedition, my friend Putney, who was killed, had a premonition of disaster to himself and dreaded to go on that

march. He had always been ready for anything that might come up. He did not sham sickness but was sad, feeling that he would never come back.

Welcome J. Johnson of Company F[13]

Years later when Hervey Shepard Johnson died, a newspaper account recalled his dash after the rebels described above.

It was during the so-called railroad fight that the incident occurred. A number of rebel prisoners escaped and volunteers were called for to recapture them. Among the first to respond were H. Shepard and Welcome

Carte de visite, Edmund Buxton Johnson, ca. autumn of 1862, photographed in his uniform of the Forty-fifth Massachusetts by Heard & Moseley, Cartes de Visite, 10 Tremont Row, Boston. Courtesy of Nahant Public Library.

Johnson, brothers. The path lay right across the fire of the rebels' entrenched position, where, in the distance, the prisoners could be seen making for their comrades. The Union party performed their work and returned with every escaped prisoner, receiving hearty commendations from their commander. Later in the day in an assault upon the rebels' entrenched position, the Johnson brothers with their comrades passed over the same ground, then a scene of carnage and death caused by the rain of rebel bullets that the volunteer squad had so miraculously escaped. At the regimental reunions comrades of the Nahant men often spoke of this act of bravery.[14]

Slouch hat with plume and Forty-fifth Regimental badge worn by Edmund Buxton Johnson during the New Bern campaign. Nahant Historical Society.

Certainly, the battles and movements around New Bern did not reach the scale of Antietam, Gettysburg, Vicksburg, or Atlanta, and until Sherman's arrival in 1865, were considered by the War Department as minor operations. New Bern has suffered even more so in subsequent history, barely rating a brief mention in the most thorough Civil War history and generally forgotten by most. But whether a soldier dies in a major battle or a small skirmish, the sacrifice is the same. As Welcome Johnson observed, "it mattered not how humble our position, we were in the service of our country, engaged in the greatest conflict between right and wrong the Western Hemisphere had ever experienced." For the men of Nahant who served for those nine months in 1862–63, their experience and contribution to the war to preserve their country would remain a source of pride for the rest of their lives.

13. Mann, *History of the Forty-fifth Regiment*, 411–14.

14. Lynn *Daily Evening Item*, May 16, 1905, Johnson obituary.

four

THE HOME FRONT

WHEN THE WAR BEGAN IN APRIL 1861, A GREAT WAVE OF ENTHUSIASM
swept through Nahant. While Luther Dame drilled the Home Guard,
watchers kept a lookout for enemy ships. Nahant would not be caught
unprepared. Let the rebels come if they dared! A cannon was set up
on Fox Hill to defend the peninsula from attack. On July Fourth,
the Ellsworth Cadets came to Nahant by invitation and impulsively
charged the cannon. However, they were met with stout fortitude by
the Home Guard and defeated. It is obvious the realities of war had not
been revealed. The first battle had yet to be fought; the first casualty
list had not been printed. Nahant, like the rest of the nation, soon
would settle down to the grim business of fighting the most deadly and
difficult foe they had ever faced—for Americans fought themselves.[1]

What sobered Nahant in the summer of 1861 had nothing to do with
the war—it was fire. First, on Tuesday, July 9, just two days before
the Longfellow family made its summer move to Nahant, Fanny
Longfellow's dress caught fire in their Cambridge home. Severely
burned, she died the next day. On Saturday, after her funeral, her
brokenhearted father died as well. Longfellow, suffering from burns
he received trying to douse the flames, as well as extreme grief, did
not come to Nahant until much later in the season. Many in the town
mourned the loss of Fanny. Then, on September 11, fire claimed
another victim well known to Nahanters—the great hotel built by
Colonel Perkins in 1823. From all accounts, the blaze was spectacular,

Frances "Fanny"
Elizabeth Appleton
Longfellow, by Black
and Batchelder,
ca. 1861, beloved
scholar wife of
Henry Wadsworth
Longfellow, shortly
before her accidental
death due to
severe fire burns.
Courtesy National
Park Service
Longfellow National
Historic Site.

and the fire departments of Nahant and Lynn could do nothing to stop it. Fire brought Nahant back to reality.[2]

The war continued, and Nahant did its part to raise soldiers. In 1861, a town meeting pledged financial support for the families of soldiers. This became official at the annual town meeting in March 1862. The town voted $300 to aid the families of soldiers and a $200 bounty for all soldiers who enlisted. As discussed in chapter 2, wealthy summer residents would add to this in July, and in August, the town would extend the bounty to nine-month volunteers.[3] In 1862, the town paid bounties of $200 to George Stone, Marcellus Kidder, Alexander Webber, Daniel Seavey, John Wheeler, George C. Neal, Charles H. Palmer, Edward J. Johnson, Edmund B. Johnson, Lorenzo Whitney, Charles N. Babb, James Campbell, William H. Perry, and John Simpson. They paid Sidney C. Johnson $60 and Luther S. Johnson $80. Another notation refers to "treasury notes to sundry individuals for bounty, $1,060." The total bounty money paid out by Nahant in 1862 was $4,200.[4]

The families of the following soldiers received support that year: Patrick Riley—$144; George F. Newhall—$24; Alexander Webber—$30; George P. Stone— $84.40; Edward J. Johnson— $44.57; and Charles H. Palmer— $66. Patrick Riley and George F.

1. Paterson & Seaburg, *Nahant*, 141–42.

2. Paterson & Seaburg, *Nahant*, 142–43.

3. Wilson, *Annals*, 103.

4. *Tenth Annual Report of the Town of Nahant, February 28, 1863* (Lynn, MA, 1863), 7.

Newhall had died, and George P. Stone was wounded. In all, the town provided $92.97 more than the $300 appropriated in March.[5]

Even the School Committee Report for February 1862 was colored by the war. First, one of their teachers, Luther Dame, who had taught seven years with "such uniform satisfaction" (and who had drilled the Home Guard since April 1861), was commissioned a captain in the Eleventh Massachusetts Volunteer Infantry. Dame's timing was poor, as the report says "it consequently devolved upon the committee to fill his post at this most unfortunate period, since it is the close of this term that the annual examination takes place." But the war also caused the School Committee to reflect on the education of their children.

> One of the many lessons taught us by the present public disorder in our country is, that our young men should be instructed in some of the elementary principles of the military art; for whilst we do not forget that peace is the true glory especially of a government like ours, yet our unhappy experience proves that even the most highly favored nations cannot expect entire exemption from war. Many of the elements of military knowledge would be useful to the citizens in the practical duties of life in time of peace, beside the general truth, that the recognized ability of a people to wage successful war is the most likely condition to ensure lasting peace.

What were these "elementary principles of the military art"? They included physiology, particularly the development of muscle and limbs; treatment of simple fractures and wounds; resuscitation from drowning; guarding against sunstroke; properties of common articles of food and its preparation; familiarity with horses, to include selection, training, care and use; instructions on gunnery; and the measurement of heights and distances. There is no indication that this

5. *Tenth Annual Report*, 6.

new and demanding curriculum was actually inflicted on the school children of Nahant.[6]

The year 1862 was perhaps the most difficult for Nahant. Not only did most of their men leave that year, but also the war and the destruction of the hotel reduced the number of summer visitors. On July 16, a still grieving Longfellow wrote a letter in which he described Nahant as "very sad this summer; 'remote, unfriended, melancholy, slow.'"[7] On July 19, he recorded in his journal that "Nahant is very solitary and deserted this year. I stood looking a day or two ago . . . down at the steamboat landing opposite. Not a fishing boat; not a human being in sight. Then the ghostly little steamer comes in, and the phantoms go over the hill toward the ruins of the old hotel, and all is still and lonely again."[8]

Another summer resident, Anna Jones Dunn Phillips, recorded on August 9 the departure of Lorenzo Whitney for the war. "Lorenzo left & I am not sorry." Although she liked Lorenzo (he apparently did handiwork for her), she knew the country needed him. On August 20, she "called at Mrs Hunt's & at Mrs Whitney's, Loren's mother." The next day she would write, "I hope to get Loren back." In early September, she wrote of the discouraging news from the front. "Everybody is feeling very sad about our army having constantly to retreat. Everything looks very dark." The following December, Anna would learn of the death of a relative on the battlefield and echoed the feelings of many who learned such news. "The shock is dreadful!" she wrote, "Oh God, support and comfort me."[9]

That December, Longfellow recorded going to see the ironclad ship the *Nahant*, which had docked in Boston. The town was well known among Navy circles it seems. The *Nahant* was a monitor and served with the South Atlantic Squadron off South Carolina. It participated

6. *Ninth Annual Report of the School Committee of the Town of Nahant, February 28, 1862* (Lynn, MA, 1862).

7. Paterson & Seaburg, *Nahant*, 146.

8. *Life of Longfellow*, Vol. III, 16.

9. Diary of Anna Jones Dunn Phillips, Nahant Historical Society.

in the attack on Morris Island on August 17, 1863, where it fired 446 shots and suffered 69 hits. The ship operated off Forts Sumter and Wagner and Sullivan's Island.[10]

Also in December, a Nahant resident wrote a letter to Edmund Johnson, then serving with the Forty-fifth Massachusetts Volunteers. The letter reveals that Nahant was less lively than in the past and discusses the news of the war (what we today would call armchair quarterbacking). It also shows that many northerners supported the war to preserve the country but thought little more for the slaves than their southern opponents.

The letter is dated December 1, 1862, and the writer, a Johnson (the first name is obscure), told Edmund that the town had to furnish two more men for nine months, and that they will be drafted if they do not volunteer. "They seem to want to get all of the able-bodied

men that there [are] in Massachusetts." He followed this with complaints that Boston was not doing its share in sending men to the war. "But this is only one instance among ten thousand that shows the rottenness of this *Nigger Admiring Nation*." Just a short time before the letter was written, Abraham Lincoln had removed the popular General George B. McClellan from command of the Army of the Potomac for not pursuing the rebels more aggressively. Lincoln had replaced McClellan with General Ambrose Burnside.

10. Charles Boynton, *The History of the Navy During the Rebellion* (New York, 1867), 212–13.

Carte de visite, Jessie Ann Benton Frémont. This author and wife of John C. Frémont was the chief promoter of her husband's career. Photographed ca. 1862 by E. Anthony, 501 Broadway, NY. Courtesy of Nahant Public Library.

Johnson had some comments about that change. "The long heels begin to show a disposition to waver a little now that their *Beautiful Burnside dose* [*sic*] not move any faster. Perhaps they will see . . . after it is too late that McClellan did about right not to move his army until it was in condition."

Johnson told Edmund that Charles Warren Johnson's body had been returned and buried the day before.[11] He also said that all the soldiers were missed at Thanksgiving. "We can well say that Nahant is as dead as *Chelsea* . . . I thought it was always dull enough but this winter will beat all winters before this. . . . The [church] meetings down there begin to look rather slim. We miss you in the *choir*." Finally, Johnson kidded Edmund about his present circumstances. "How does hard tack go, [and] salt horse, as I take it you don't have any feather beds to sleep on, eh, nothing but the soft side."[12]

Life would begin to return to Nahant in 1863 as the summer people found their way back to the peninsula. The Palfrys noticed that the steamboat was running on a regular basis once again. "People are pouring in droves to the boat . . . and the fine weather this week tempts beaucoup de monde to picnic on the hotel grounds."[13] The town also gained an illustrious resident, albeit for a short time. General John C. Frémont was one of the great enigmas of American history. There is no question that he was brave, even headstrong, and he rarely suffered from indecision. But Frémont was driven by a passionate ambition to gain as much power and public adoration as possible, and he used every opportunity, every means available, including disobedience, disregard for subordinates, and all the considerable political influence and protection provided by his marriage, to achieve it. In the end, what mattered most to John C. Frémont was John C. Frémont.

Frémont was a household name even before the war. He led mapping expeditions in the west in the early 1840s. Sent to California during

11. He had died in the navy. See chapter 2.

12. Letter to Edmund Johnson, "Johnson Family" file, Nahant Historical Society.

13. Paterson & Seaburg, *Nahant*, 146.

Previous spread:
Left: Photograph, USS *Nahant*, showing this monitor out of service at the New York Navy Yard between the end of the Civil War and the start of the Spanish-American War. Nahant Historical Society.

Right: Photograph, USS *Nahant*. This 1,335-ton *Passaic* class monitor, popularly known as *an ironclad*, was built at the Boston Navy Yard in 1862. She was part of the South Atlantic Squadron, which attacked Fort Sumter at Charleston, South Carolina, April 7, 1862. Nahant Historical Society.

the Mexican War, he exceeded his orders and prematurely raised the American flag, claiming the territory for the United States. Although he initially caused problems by doing this, the Anglo-Californians loved him for it and selected him as one of their senators. He also discovered gold on his California ranch, which made him wealthy. His marriage to Jessie Benton, daughter of the powerful Senator Thomas Hart Benton, helped him a great deal. In 1856, he became the first presidential candidate for the Republican Party ("Free Soil, Free Speech, Frémont!") and lost.

At the start of the Civil War, he helped save Missouri for the Union and was Ulysses S. Grant's commander. He had a personal bodyguard of three hundred picked men and an entourage of staff officers, among them Hungarians and Italians with outrageous titles. As in the Mexican War, he once again exceeded his authority.[14] Frémont issued his own emancipation order freeing the slaves. This was still 1861, and the border slave states, particularly Kentucky, were still deciding whether to secede or not. Frémont's order pushed them southward. Lincoln's primary concern at that point was to prevent more states from seceding, so he suggested that Frémont withdraw the order. Frémont wrote a letter refusing the president's request, and his wife, Jessie, personally delivered it to Lincoln. The interview was not pleasant. Lincoln hardly got a word in edgewise as Jessie extolled the virtues of John C. Frémont, and when the president refused to worship the hero himself, she left in a huff. Lincoln ordered Frémont to withdraw his order and then in October relieved him of his command. (The officer who delivered this order had to sneak his way through Frémont's army of bodyguards.)[15]

Frémont continued to serve, first in the Mississippi River theater, then in command of a small force operating in the Shenandoah Valley against Stonewall Jackson in the spring of 1862, a most unfortunate time and place for Union generals. When General John Pope was placed in command over him, Frémont sent a letter of resignation in protest. Lincoln accepted it.

14. Lincoln, to his regret, had given Frémont carte blanche to do whatever he wanted.

15. Foote, *The Civil War, A Narrative: Fort Sumter to Perryville*, 89–99.

Without a military position, Frémont hovered at the periphery of events waiting for his chance. During the summer of 1863, the Frémonts were staying in New York City. When the draft riots erupted, he placed thirty-five armed guards in the lobby of the hotel. After the riots, Frémont and Jessie sought a place of retreat from the turmoil. That retreat was Nahant.

They arrived at the end of July and took the cottage next to Longfellow. They would spend this summer and the next in Nahant. By all accounts, Jessie fit right in with the Nahant summer people, but Frémont did not. Anna Palfry wrote in August 1863 that "after church in the morning we called on the Frémonts and arranged with them to take seats in our pew in the afternoon. To my disappointment the Gen. was out but we saw his wife 'Our Jessie,' a comely, stout, pleasant looking middle-aged woman."[16] Frederic Tudor believed Frémont was "not very popular. He will not last in this neighborhood."[17] In 1864, the General had Longfellow's children arrested for swimming on "his beach." The charges were dropped when it was pointed out that "his beach" was not really his. A. A. Lawrence recorded that "General Frémont appears to be inefficient. Assumes great state, rides in a coach and four. How fortunate he was not made President of the United States."[18]

A second chance at that office came to Frémont in 1864 when the radicals in the Republican Party chose him as their candidate for president. His Nahant neighbor Longfellow wrote in his journal "what merry times I shall have with my neighbor the Frémonts during the campaign for the Presidency not meaning to vote for him."[19] When the Democrats nominated George McClellan as a "peace" candidate at the same time that William T. Sherman captured Atlanta, Republicans urged Frémont to get out of the campaign in order not to split the party vote. John Greenleaf Whittier, a family friend, visited him in

---

16. Hannah Palfry Ayer, *A Legacy of New England: Letters of the Palfry Family* (Boston, 1950), 332.

17. Paterson & Seaburg, *Nahant*, 147.

18. Paterson & Seaburg, *Nahant*, 147, 149.

19. Paterson & Seaburg, *Nahant*, 148–49.

Nahant in September to convince him not to run. After much soul-searching, Frémont withdrew from the race on September 22 but not without a final jab at Lincoln. "I consider that his administration has been politically, militarily, and financially a failure, and that its necessary continuance a cause of regret for the country."[20]

The Frémonts left Nahant that fall never to return. The little peninsula was just too small to contain Frémont's ego. After the war, Frémont suffered severe financial reverses, but Jessie's writing and his army pension kept them above water. He died in 1890 and she in 1902.

With the hotel gone, the Nahant social scene shifted to the war and Sanitary parties. For those not able to don a uniform and fight the enemy in person, the expression of support for the war usually focused on helping the soldiers. On an informal basis, mothers, wives, and sweethearts sent their men the extra items they needed for their comfort, but those without a relative in the war satisfied this impulse

Photograph, Frémont Cottage, now 171 Nahant Road, viewed from the back of 35 Cliff Street. Nahant Historical Society.

20. Paterson & Seaburg, *Nahant*, 149; Shelby Foote, *The Civil War, A Narrative: Red River to Appomattox* (New York, 1974), 559.

with more formal organizations and activities. Three organizations in particular formed to supply the needs of the soldiers: soldier's aid societies, the Christian Commission, and the United States Sanitary Commission.

Local soldier's aid societies sprang up throughout the north to provide for the soldiers; one of the more prominent was the New England Soldier's Aid Society. Women enthusiastically jumped into sewing and knitting. In the spring of 1861, the most common article was the "havelock," named after British General Henry Havelock, who was connected to it through sketches of the India Mutiny. The havelock was a linen or cotton covering that slipped over the forage cap and had a large flap hanging down in the back to protect the wearer from the hot sun. Northern women knew it was hot in the south, so they were sure their men needed these. In May 1861, a New York sewing circle made up twelve hundred havelocks and presented them to the Sixty-ninth New York. Students in one Massachusetts academy made 138 before the end of June.

The soldiers were deluged with havelocks and found it very amusing. They rarely used them for protection because they not only blocked the sun, but also any refreshing breeze as well, which made the soldiers even hotter. Most were torn up for musket cleaning patches. However, the women learned from this and began to provide more practical articles, like extra shirts, socks, gloves, mittens, etc. As knitting and sewing are tasks that enable women to converse, they usually met together. Thus, the production of shirts and socks became an important social function during the war.[21]

These soldier's aid societies were essentially local organizations. On the national level, the Christian Commission guarded the spiritual welfare of the men, providing them with bibles, hymnals, and religious tracts. Perhaps the most famous civilian support group was the United States Sanitary Commission. Formed in May 1861 under the leadership of Reverend Henry Whitney Bellows, who was known to vacation and preach at Nahant, the Sanitary Commission took on the task of coordinating the soldier support efforts. The Commission was divided into five sections: the Sanitary Inspection viewed the conditions of the military camps; General Relief coordinated the distribution of food, clothing, and hospital supplies (much of it coming from those local groups sewing, knitting, and baking their hearts out); Special Relief provided homes for recruits, soldiers on furlough, or any soldier needing a temporary roof; Field Relief packed their tents into wagons and followed the armies, providing whatever they could; and, finally, the Auxiliary Relief Corps served in hospitals. Ten "headquarters," including one in Boston, funneled the clothing, food, bandages, etc., to the army. One estimate placed the value of these contributed articles at $15 million. The money for the organization was raised through subscriptions and "Sanitary Fairs." Some of the fairs in major cities involved thousands of people, but even small communities made contributions. The U.S. Sanitary Commission raised through these various means over $4.8 million and dispersed $4.5 million to the war effort.[22]

That Nahant was active in these home front activities is very evident. Summer resident Mary A. P. Russell returned from Paris at the start of the war. She recorded, "we at once entered into all that was doing, sewed and toiled for the soldiers, helped Mrs. Otis in her great work . . . I worked with her and Mrs. Lowell, was equipped with apron, shears and thimble—and we heard that the soldiers cleaned their guns with the cotton havelocks we toiled to make. I remember Miss Caroline Crowninshield rushing in and telling us that our soldiers were bombarding Maryland—in her excitement she took the state for the city of Baltimore."[23] Anna Palfry, another summer resident, wrote to her brother in August 1862 that "twice a week there are Sanitary parties in the forenoon, to sew for the soldiers. They are patronized by young and old of both sexes." One such party that summer had over sixty people and musical entertainment.[24]

21. Mary Elizabeth Massey, *Women in the Civil War* (1966, reprint Lincoln, NE, 1994), 31–32.

22. Lord, *They Fought for the Union*, 131–32; Paterson & Seaburg, *Nahant*, 148.

23. Mary A. P. Russell, "Past and Present from 1826–1911: Record of My Happy Life" (unpublished manuscript, Nahant Historical Society), 10–11.

As the war went on, the Sanitary parties became more elaborate. In 1863, Nahant's summer population began to reappear, and more people meant larger and livelier Sanitary parties. Anna Palfry wrote that on August 12 she attended "such a charming Sanitary tea party . . . at Mrs. Chadwick's . . . there was such a fine band playing so much delightful music." Rain forced the party inside, but the band continued to play while "people walked and sat and danced and drank tea and ate cake and listened to the music."[25] The *Lynn Reporter* noted that twelve- to fourteen-year-old girls held a Sanitary Fair in Nahant in late September. They raised $120 and ran out of supplies because so many people attended. "Mrs. General Frémont went away empty-handed, being too late."[26] The following year, a play was written and performed at the town school that caused a great deal of excitement. The theme of the play (there appeared to be no real plot) chastised those who did no work for the war effort. The "Goddess America" and a "wounded soldier" showed them the error of their ways.[27]

There is no doubt that many home front people experienced pressure to contribute more and more. Anna Palfry related one incident in the summer of 1863: "Willy Paige walked with me and asked me point blank why I did not go away as a hospital nurse. I have never looked upon that as my mission, and I was about as unprepared to reply as if he had asked me why I did not go to Patagonia. I told him we had had a hospital at home and that a great deal had been said of the unwillingness of the government to accept the services of amateurs."[28]

Throughout the war, the town of Nahant continued to provide financial support for the soldiers and families. In March 1863, they voted $300 more for aid to soldiers' families. In that fiscal year, they would pay $114 to Ann Riley, Patrick's widow, $35 to John Wheeler, $51 to Alexander Webber, $36.58 to Edward J. Johnson, $144 to

24. Paterson & Seaburg, *Nahant*, 148.

25. Paterson & Seaburg, *Nahant*, 148.

26. *Lynn Reporter*, September 26, 1863.

27. Paterson & Seaburg, *Nahant*, 148.

28. Ayer, *A Legacy of New England*, 333.

George P. Stone, and $60 to Charles H. Palmer. This totals $140.58 above the $300 appropriated. The following year, the town voted to continue aid, remit taxes for all volunteers, and provide a $125 bounty to fill new quotas. In March 1865, they reported aid paid out the previous year to George P. Stone ($36) and Alexander Webber ($52) and recruiting expenses totaling $873. In 1865, the town paid out $39

to Alexander Webber. One source indicates that the total expenditure by the town during the war exceeded $6,500.[29]

Like most communities in America, the town of Nahant was deeply touched by the Civil War. The war not only removed many of their men, it required sacrifice by those left behind, the sacrifice of time, labor, and money. The people of Nahant, both part-time and full-time residents, came through. After all, the time to sew a shirt, work a Sanitary Fair, or pay the increase in taxes to support the family of a volunteer compared little to the prospect of death and wounds experienced by the men in uniform. If they could use the support to provide entertainment and diversion, even better, but they never forgot the serious purpose behind the parties. This care and concern for those directly affected by the war would continue in the postwar years as well.

29. Wilson, *Annals*, 104–5; *Annual Town Reports*, 1864, 1865, 1866.

Print of a painting of John Charles Frémont, ca. February 23, 1859, by John Chester Buttre, 18 Franklin Street, New York. Renowned explorer of the West, Frémont was nicknamed "The Pathfinder" and was later a politician with designs on the presidency. Courtesy of the Library of Congress.

None of the returned soldiers belonging to Nahant have been
guilty of any crime since their return home. Their characters were
unimpeachable before they enlisted in the army, and they still
continue the same, and are in every respect good citizens.

—W. H. Johnson, Chairman, Selectmen of Nahant
Massachusetts Adjutant-General's Report for 1866

GREAT CELEBRATION AND RELIEF PASSED OVER THE COUNTRY in April 1865,
tinged with grief over the assassination of Abraham Lincoln. People in
Nahant and elsewhere began to put their lives back together, as in the
following months the three-year volunteer regiments returned to the
state and were mustered out. The country entered what became known
as the Reconstruction Period, when much of the political energies of
the national government focused on bringing the southern states back
into the union and enforcing the provisions of the Fourteenth and
Fifteenth Amendments. During that time, the South remained under
military occupation. In 1877, a political compromise involving the
election of Rutherford B. Hayes and the removal of troops from the
South ended Reconstruction. According to standard history books,
the country turned its attention to the settlement of the West and the
Indian wars against the plains and mountain tribes. The United States

Carte de visite,
Sophia Dennis
Hood (Mrs.
Elbridge G. Hood),
ca. 1865. This
resourceful woman
used her extensive
dressmaking skills
to augment her
family income
when her husband's
health continued
to decline postwar
because of wounds
received at the
Battle of Antietam.
Courtesy of Nahant
Public Library.

also experienced tremendous economic expansion that became known as "The Gilded Age" and entered the world with the Spanish-American War, imperialism, and Teddy Roosevelt (who visited Nahant in 1902[1]).

In looking to the past, it is easy to compartmentalize history, to break it down into phases and eras, each separate and distinct, usually lasting about thirty years. Recently, it is common to refer to "generations," but the reference has contracted so that a generation becomes a twenty-year period, even a decade. Once past, it is no longer a force but a curiosity. However, people live much longer than ten, twenty, or thirty years. Youths grow into middle age and take the reins of society from their fathers. So it was with the Civil War "generation." The young men who went to war would live another forty or fifty years. In that time, they would own the stores, farms, and factories; they would participate in local, state, and national government; and they would become the controllers and leaders of their society. For those who lived with it, the Civil War would never become a curiosity. They would never be conscious of entering a new distinct historical era. The Civil War would remain a central episode in their lives and affect their thinking and actions, and thus their society and culture.

Nahant veterans returned to resume their place in the town, and many of them would eventually achieve prominence in the community.

Watercolor *USS Octorara* (1862–66) by Alex Stuart. Charles Quimby served from 1864 to 1865 on this 981-ton "double-ender" side-wheel gunboat during its Gulf of Mexico blockade duty. Courtesy of the Navy Art Collection and the U.S. Naval Historical Center, Photo # 86354-KN.

1. Paterson & Seaburg, *Nahant*, 202–7.

Naturally, the Johnson family continued to be significant. Edward J. Johnson owned a fish market. He would serve on the Board of Selectmen for the town of Nahant, as well as two terms as a representative in the Massachusetts General Court. Edward was also the first chief engineer of the Nahant Fire Department. His interest in the community and local history was keen. He contributed a section entitled "History of the Town of Nahant" for the published *History of Essex County*, and he wrote numerous genealogical articles.

Luther Scott Johnson did very well in the shoe business and manufacturing. He was vice president and director of the Security Trust Co., a member of the Investment Committee of the Investment Institution of Savings, and president of Lynn Hospital. Edmund Buxton Johnson lived on Nahant Road and ran a boarding house. He was a selectman for three years and town treasurer and served on the Nahant School Board for eighteen years. Edmund was also a trustee of the Nahant Independent Church. Hervey S. Johnson worked in hay and grain and then manufactured duck (canvas) and leather coats in Lynn. He served on the Nahant School Committee and was trustee of the Village Church. Edwin W. Johnson served as postmaster and storeowner for many years, and Welcome J. Johnson owned a coal and ice business.

Carte de visite, Luther Scott Johnson, postwar in 1866. Photographer: Richardson—Lima, state unknown. Courtesy of Nahant Public Library.

Other resident veterans made their contribution to the community as well. Charles H. Palmer, living on Summer Street Court, continued his profession of carpenter, and William Johnson continued to be a mariner. Michael Mitchell, one of the men with an oh-so-short career in the Nineteenth U.S. Infantry, lived in Nahant as a liquor dealer and saloon keeper. John Waters, who served in the navy during the war, worked as a laborer for the town. Although we cannot be sure what they did for work, the other Nahant veterans, Elbridge Hood, John Wheeler, Sidney C. Johnson, Arthur Bulfinch, and Lorenzo

2. "Soldiers Bio" file, NHS.

Whitney, all contributed to Nahant simply by being members of the community.[2]

However, it was not only the wartime residents who helped Nahant toward its future, but also veterans who moved there in the years after the war. The Civil War produced a certain restlessness among many who served, a restlessness that produced movement. A great number followed the railroad to the West, but others moved to new homes in the East. Whether through restlessness or economic opportunity, several Civil War veterans moved to Nahant. They were welcomed as comrades and equals, and a few made significant contributions.

Thomas J. Cusick had an exciting time in the war. Born in Brookline, Cusick listed himself as a butcher when he enlisted in the Tenth Battery, Massachusetts Light Artillery, on February 18, 1864. The Tenth Massachusetts Battery had originally been raised in 1862. By the time Cusick joined, the battery was assigned to the Second Corps, Army of the Potomac.

In May 1864, Ulysses S. Grant began his long campaign against Lee, which resulted in a series of brutal engagements beginning with the

Watercolor by Erik Heyl, 1952, of *Totten*, renamed *Chesapeake*, painted for his book *Early American Steamers*, Volume III. This 460-ton wooden steamship rescued the crew of the USS *Caleb Cushing*, among them Andrew Fuller, when captured by the Confederate raider *Archer*, June 26, 1863, in the Gulf of Maine. Courtesy of the U.S. Naval Historical Center, Photo # NH 67079.

Wilderness, followed by the siege of Petersburg, and ending with the Appomattox campaign the following year. The Second Corps participated in almost all of them. In fact, Cusick and the Tenth Battery found itself in eighteen engagements. The battery was hard hit at Reams Station on August 25, 1864. The Second Corps had been tearing up sections of the Weldon Railroad when the Confederates launched a surprise attack. The result was the worst defeat of the whole war for the proud Second Corps.[3] The Second Corps's historian describes the Tenth Massachusetts Battery firing canister point blank at the charging rebels. The battery lost all its guns, five killed, four wounded, nineteen prisoners, and fifty-four horses.

Among the prisoners was Thomas Cusick. Cusick spent six months in Libbey Prison in Richmond before being paroled in December. He

Photograph, USS *Niagara* (1857–85), a 5,540-ton (displacement) steam screw frigate shown off Boston, Massachusetts, in 1863. James Timmins served aboard while this vessel was often the flagship of the East Gulf Blockading Squadron. Courtesy of the U.S. Naval Historical Center, Photo # 75895.

---

3. Many of its regiments had been gutted after months of constant campaigning, and the ranks were filled with raw recruits and draftees.

4. "Soldier Bio" file, NHS; *Mass. Soldiers*, 10th Battery, Mass. Lt. Art.; Francis Walker, *History of the Second Corps in the Army of the Potomac* (New York, 1887), 591–94.

Patrick Lenehan's rifle musket and bayonet, ca. 1864. Note the religious medal with prayer attached to the shoulder sling swivel ring. The renowned Springfield Armory of Massachusetts, which still stands today as a National Historic Site, made this U.S. Model 1863, type II rifle musket a.k.a. Model 1864, one of 255,040 made. Private Collection.

rejoined the Tenth, now refitted with new equipment, and served until the battery was mustered out in June 1865. Moving to Nahant after the war, Cusick would open a grocery store, become chief of the Fire Department, and serve twenty-five years as postmaster. He lived at 165 Willow Road.[4]

Alfred A. Barnes was born in Henniker, New Hampshire, and joined the Eleventh New Hampshire Volunteer Infantry on August 14, 1862. The Eleventh joined the Ninth Corps that fall and was assigned to the same brigade as the Thirty-fifth Massachusetts. The regiment participated at Fredericksburg and then went with the Ninth Corps to Mississippi and Tennessee. In 1864, it returned east to participate with Grant's campaign against Lee, but Alfred Barnes was not with it. He was transferred to the VRC on January 15. Barnes mustered out of the army on July 5, 1865. When he moved to Nahant, he became the first custodian of the Valley Road School and a police officer for the town. As we shall see, Barnes would play a significant role in the story of the Nahant veterans.[5]

Robert Lang Cochrane served with the 139th New York Volunteer Infantry from August 22, 1862, until he was discharged in May 1865 with a wound in the left knee. Cochrane's connection to Nahant came by way of marriage. He married Margaret Johnson and moved to his wife's town where he became superintendent of the Nahant Water Department, a position he held for forty years.[6]

George W. Kibbey was a shoemaker who enlisted in the Forty-second Massachusetts Volunteer Infantry on August 20, 1862. The Forty-second served in the New Orleans theater and was part of the force that attacked Galveston, Texas, on January 1, 1863. Trapped by a rebel counterattack, the colonel and three companies of the Forty-second were captured. Among them was George Kibbey. Although

5. "Soldier Bio" file, NHS; Leander W. Cogswell, *A History of the Eleventh New Hampshire Regiment Volunteer Infantry in the Rebellion War, 1861–65* (Concord, NH, 1891).

6. "Soldier Bio" file, NHS.

paroled within a few months, Kibbey was discharged in August for medical reasons. He moved to Nahant in the 1890s and ran a stable on Wharf Street. He lived at 354 Nahant Road (just down from Elbridge Hood who lived at 368 Nahant Road). Kibbey became known for the annual party he gave on Washington's Birthday, which was also the anniversary of the opening of his stable. One newspaper reporter wrote that "a lunch consisting of steamed clams, sardines, crackers and 'sarsaparilla' was served to all comers . . . About 100 guests called to extend congratulations during the day."[7]

Patrick Henry Winn was another veteran who served in a Forty-second Massachusetts, but the Forty-second Massachusetts Militia, called up for one hundred days between July 8 and November 8, 1864. Winn moved to Nahant and lived there until 1898. He worked as a plumber out of his shop on Willow Road. Dwight Lamphear was born in Lanesboro, Massachusetts, and served in the Second Massachusetts Heavy Artillery, which spent much of its time in garrisons around New Bern. Lamphear was discharged from New Bern because of disability on July 28, 1864. After the war, he moved to Nahant and ran a lodging house.[8]

Patrick Lenehan was born in Ireland in 1845 and in 1863 enlisted in the Fifty-sixth Massachusetts, the same regiment as James Campbell

Watercolor, *USS Kearsarge* (as she was during Civil War service) by Clary Ray, ca. 1890s. Michael John Sweeney served on this 1,550-ton *Mohican*-class steam sloop of war in 1862. Courtesy of the U.S. Naval Historical Center, Photo # KN-571.

7. "Soldier Bio" file, NHS; *Mass. Soldiers*, 42nd Mass. Vol. Inf.; Lynn *Daily Evening Item*, February 24, 1908.

8. "Soldier Bio" file, NHS; *Mass. Soldiers*, 42nd Mass. Vol. Militia, 2nd Mass. Hvy. Art.

Photograph, USS *Fort Donelson*, at anchor, ca. 1864–65. Michael John Sweeney served with a rating of fireman first class on this 642-ton iron-hulled side-wheel steam gunboat, formerly the Confederate blockade-runner, *Robert E. Lee*. Courtesy of the U.S. Naval Historical Center, Photo # NH 53934.

(see chapter 2). Although this was a veteran regiment, not all the members of the Fifty-sixth Massachusetts had seen service before. Lenehan was eighteen when he joined and had apparently tried to enlist earlier in the war, but his young age prevented it. With the Fifty-sixth Massachusetts, he participated in Grant's campaign against Lee, starting with the Wilderness in May of 1864, through the siege of Petersburg, and ending with the pursuit to Appomattox. He mustered out of the service as a corporal in July 1865. Lenehan moved to Nahant in 1874 and worked for the town's highway department.[9]

Frank Deshon's move to Nahant was gradual. Deshon enlisted in the Thirty-eighth Massachusetts Volunteer Infantry on August 20, 1862,

9. "Soldier Bio" file, NHS; *Mass. Soldiers*, 56th Mass. Vol. Inf. The name is often spelled "Linehan" and is spelled that way in *Mass. Soldiers*. An article in the Lynn *Item* on April 4, 1927, made an error concerning his war record. The reporter wrote that Lenehan was at "Bull Run, Cold Harbor, Wilderness, the Battle of Spotsylvania and finished his service at Appomattox." The Fifty-sixth was raised after Second Bull Run, so this is clearly wrong. Whether Lenehan's memory was at fault or the reporter got his facts wrong is unknown. However, since the reporter listed Cold Harbor before the chronologically earlier Wilderness, we can assume that the reporter's knowledge of the Civil War was superficial at best.

and stayed with the regiment until the end of the war. As detailed in chapter 2, the Thirty-eighth was well traveled, serving in New Orleans, the Shenandoah Valley in 1864, and with Schofield's force in the New Bern to Goldsboro campaign in 1865. After the war, Deshon worked in a lasting jack factory in Saugus, Massachusetts. In 1889 or 1890, he opened a summer restaurant in Nahant called the Greenwood Cottage Cafe. The business was apparently successful, which enabled him to move to Nahant in 1896 or 1897. A fellow member of the Thirty-eighth Massachusetts, Charles Quimby, also moved to Nahant, making his home at 13 Irving Way. Quimby enlisted on August 11, 1862, and served with the Thirty-eighth Massachusetts until July 1864 when, for some unknown reason, he was transferred to the navy. It certainly was not owing to prior experience. Quimby listed himself as a farmer living in Lynn when he enlisted. In the navy, he served on the *Portsmouth* and the *Octorara* until discharged at the end of the war. Quimby worked as a painter in Nahant.[10]

Other navy veterans also settled in Nahant. Andrew Fuller was born in Nova Scotia in 1831 and moved to Portland, Maine, at the age of sixteen. He joined the navy and was assigned to the revenue cutter *Caleb Cushing*. Fuller and the *Caleb Cushing* were involved in a little known but exciting episode of the war. The captain of the ship died, and the *Caleb Cushing* put into Portland, Maine, for the burial. The date was June 26, 1863. While half the crew were on shore for the ceremony, the *Archer*, a rebel raider under the command of Charles W. Read, swept into Portland harbor and captured the *Caleb Cushing*. Placing the eighteen men on board in chains, Read left Portland with both the *Archer* and the *Caleb Cushing*. Volunteers from Portland boarded a propeller-driven steamship called the *Chesapeake* and gave chase. As the *Chesapeake* closed with Read, the rebel lieutenant released his prisoners, transferred to the *Archer*, and set fire to the *Caleb Cushing* (which subsequently blew up). The rebels attempted to escape, but the *Archer* was overtaken and captured. After the war, Fuller worked in Boston as a stevedore (longshoreman). In 1903, he moved to Nahant to help his sons run the Bass Point House.[11]

10. "Soldier Bio" file, NHS; *Mass. Soldiers*, 38th Mass. Vol. Inf.

James Timmins was born in Boston in 1823 and enlisted in the navy in 1859, so, like Mortimer L. Johnson, he was already in the service when the war began. Timmins shipped on the *Ohio*, *North Carolina*, and *Niagara* before mustering out in June 1862. One month later, he enlisted again in the navy, serving until May 1865. In that time, his ships included the *Ohio* (once again), *Housatonic*, *New Ironsides*, *Philadelphia*, and *Acacia*. After the war, he moved to Nahant and continued to be a sailor.[12]

Michael John Sweeney was born in Ireland in 1826 and immigrated to South Boston. He enlisted in the navy on January 16, 1862. He served on the famous *Kearsarge* (the ship that sank the rebel raider *Alabama*) for one month and then was discharged. He enlisted again, this time as John Sweeney, on June 20, 1864. He shipped on the *Ohio* (not at the same time as Timmins) and the *Fort Donelson* with the rate of fireman first class. He served in the navy until March 1867. He moved to Nahant in 1900 and lived at 24 Emerald Road.[13]

Albert Wilson was born at Kittery Point, Maine, in 1819. Wilson went to sea very early in life and became the captain of a ship at the age of nineteen. He sailed out of Portsmouth, New Hampshire, for twenty years. At the start of the Civil War, he was commissioned as a volunteer sailing master in the navy and was stationed at the U.S. Naval Base in Charlestown, Massachusetts. Ill health forced him to resign from this post, and he was then transferred to Fort McClary at Kittery Point to help in ship design. After the war, Joseph T. Wilson, a distant cousin, moved to Nahant and established a building business. Joseph married Albert's daughter and hired two of his sons to work for him. Albert and his wife, Calantha, followed their children to Nahant.

Two postwar residents followed Rhode Island's flag into the war, and another followed Vermont's. James Hyde Galvin enlisted in an

11. "Soldier Bio" file, NHS; *Mass. Soldiers*, Naval Service; Lynn *Daily Evening Item*, July 14, 1911.

12. "Soldier Bio" file, NHS.

13. This information and the following few paragraphs comes from the "Soldier Bio" file, NHS.

unknown Rhode Island regiment. Like Quimby, he moved to Nahant after the war and, living on Wharf Street, worked as a painter. Thomas W. Tibbets was born in Holden, Massachusetts, and was living in Lynn at the start of the war, but somehow Tibbets joined the Third Rhode Island Heavy Artillery on January 11, 1862, and mustered out on March 17, 1865. Tibbets worked as

Portrait, pastel colored photograph, Elbridge Gerry Hood. Photographed by Robert A. Wilson. Nahant Historical Society.

a last maker and moved to Nahant probably late in the nineteenth century. Benjamin F. Waldo served in the Sixteenth Vermont Volunteer Infantry and moved to Nahant sometime after the war. He lived the rest of his life on the peninsula.[14]

Fred A. Trefethan was born in Boston and enlisted in the Thirty-third Massachusetts Volunteer Infantry on August 2, 1862.[15] He stayed with the Thirty-third until the end of the war. He moved to Nahant sometime before 1890.

John H. Cummings was a shoemaker in Lynn when he enlisted in the Twenty-ninth Massachusetts Volunteer Infantry. The Twenty-

14. Brewin and Twiss missed Waldo in their research. Research on soldier burials in Greenlawn Cemetery reminded us of his service. Calantha Sears provided the information.

15. Two other men, Marcellus Kidder and George Neal, were credited from Nahant in this regiment. See chapter 2 for a description of the unit's history.

ninth originally consisted of companies of the Third and Fourth Militias that had enlisted for three years. By the end of 1861, three other companies had been raised and the regiment assigned to the Irish Brigade. This position had been intended for the Twenty-eighth Massachusetts, which was an Irish unit, but circumstances prevented this.[16] The Twenty-ninth Massachusetts was not happy with the assignment (prejudice against the Irish was very strong at the beginning of the war). They fought with the Irish Brigade through the Peninsula Campaign and Antietam, and then in the fall of 1862, they were swapped with the Twenty-eighth Massachusetts, the Irishmen finally going to the Irish Brigade and the Twenty-ninth replacing the Twenty-eighth in the Ninth Corps. The Ninth Corps then went west where it fought at Vicksburg and Jackson, Mississippi. In early 1864, most of the regiment reenlisted. The Ninth Corps was now in the East again where it joined Grant's campaign against Lee. The Twenty-ninth was at the siege of Petersburg and participated in the attack on the

16. See Patrick Riley in chapter 2.

Pen and ink sketch, ca. 1862. Richard Manning Hodges, MD, oversaw the medical headquarters of a Union Army field hospital for the Second Corps of the Army of the Potomac. It was located near the Glen-Brook Farm of Doctor Powers of York County, Virginia. Nahant Historical Society.

Crater. Cummings served with the unit until January 1, 1863, and then reenlisted in the Twenty-ninth exactly one year later. He suffered a wound in an attack on the Weldon Railroad on August 19, 1864, and was promoted to sergeant shortly before the regiment was mustered out on July 29, 1865. Cummings was living in Nahant by 1890 and worked as a shoemaker.

William Gibbs enlisted on August 20, 1862, in the Fifth Massachusetts Militia, one of the nine-month regiments that served at New Bern.[17] After the war, he became a cook at a Nahant hotel. John Trefry, a shoemaker from Lynn, also joined one of the nine-month militia regiments, the Eighth Massachusetts, in August 1862. As detailed in chapter 2, this unit had its companies dispersed for guard details around New Bern, North Carolina, and then participated briefly in the pursuit of the Army of Northern Virginia after the battle of Gettysburg. Trefry mustered out in August 1863 but reenlisted in the Fifty-ninth Massachusetts Volunteer Infantry in February 1864. This

---

17. See chapter 3.

regiment participated in the Wilderness to Cold Harbor Campaign, the siege of Petersburg, including the attack on the Crater, Weldon Railroad, and in 1865, the attack on Fort Stedman.[18] Trefry was wounded at Petersburg on June 17, 1864. After the war, June 1, 1865, he was transferred as a corporal briefly to the Fifty-seventh Massachusetts and then discharged on July 31, 1865 (apparently the government wanted the full use of John Trefry). He subsequently moved to Nahant, specifically Summer Street, and continued working as a shoemaker.

Summer residents also contributed to the number of veterans connected to Nahant. As mentioned earlier, Edward Crosby Johnson was related to the Nahant Johnsons and served with the Forty-fourth Massachusetts. Although he undoubtedly visited Nahant before the war, it is after that war that he made his mark as a summer resident. Edward had a cottage at the end of Pleasant Street. He and his brother Samuel ran the C. F. Hovey and Co. Department Store. His daughter married Curtis Guild, who became governor of Massachusetts. Admiral Henry Knox Thatcher, Mortimer Laurence Johnson's commanding officer during the war (and, from all appearances, his mentor), also became a summer resident after the war.[19] Another distinguished personage connected to the Civil War who spent summers at Nahant was General C. C. Sniffen. Sniffen was secretary to Ulysses S. Grant during the war and during Grant's presidency. He also served for a time as Army Paymaster.[20]

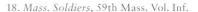

18. *Mass. Soldiers*, 59th Mass. Vol. Inf.

19. *Atlas of the Town of Nahant, Massachusetts. From Official Records, Private Plans and Actual Surveys* (G. M. Hopkins, C.E., 320 Walnut Street, Philadelphia, 1880), 27.

Dr. Richard Manning Hodges built a summer home in Nahant in 1872.[21] A professor at Harvard Medical School, Hodges had served in the war in a number of capacities. He was an acting surgeon for the Army of the Potomac in the spring of 1862 and supervised a hospital in Boston during the summer of that year. He resigned from that post to take a position as an inspector of hospitals for the United States Sanitary Commission in October 1862. Hodges was a well-known surgeon and published works on anesthesia after the war.[22]

All these men, both wartime and postwar residents, provided a living link to the Civil War. Whether their war experience had been short or long, whether they had fought in great battles or waited in garrisons, the feeling and connection to this great national trauma was the same. As they grew older and they gradually became an integral part of the economic, political, religious, and social existence of the town, so Nahant became a mirror of their beliefs and attitudes. Perhaps nothing illustrates this more than the care given those in the community whose lives were altered or even crushed by the war, particularly the support given to Ann Riley and John Simpson.

As detailed in the previous chapter, Nahant had voted to provide for families of the soldiers during the war. Among the recipients of this money had been Ann Riley, Patrick Riley's widow. Like her husband, Ann was born in Ireland, although the date is uncertain. The various census records list a startling variety of ages for Ann. She herself was probably unsure and simply guessed whenever asked. The Rileys had three children: Mary, born around 1857 or 1858; Thomas Riley, born in March 1860; and Margaret "Maggie," born in late 1861 or early 1862. The fall of 1861 was a trying time for Ann. Patrick had enlisted in the Twenty-eighth Massachusetts on October 10 and was at Camp Cameron in Cambridge. On December 16, three days after

20. "Soldier Bio" file, NHS.

21. Wilson, *Annals*, 339.

22. "Richard Manning Hodges" file, Nahant Historical Society; Military medical and surgical essays; prepared for the United States Sanitary Commission, WorldCat Libraries, http://www.worldcatlibraries.org/wcpa/top3mset/32389d93b4ce48bd.html

Patrick was sworn into federal service along with the Twenty-eighth Massachusetts, twenty-one-month-old Thomas Riley died of lung fever. Ann must have just delivered Maggie, or was close to it at the time. Then in January, her husband left for the front, never to be seen again. Of some help and comfort was the presence of Patrick's fifty-six-year-old mother, Bridget. By 1865, Bridget was gone from the household, either dead or returned to Ireland.[23]

After the war, the state of Massachusetts voted to provide for veterans and families in need. Based on set criteria, towns would pay the support and be reimbursed by the state, and any expenses above that figure would be the liability of the town. In 1866, three people received state aid: Ann Riley ($112), Elbridge Hood ($84), and John Simpson ($78). Elbridge Hood still suffered from the effects of his stomach wound, and John Simpson had been disabled by disease or injury, the exact nature unclear. The following year, all three again received state aid: Riley ($96), Hood ($72), and Simpson ($6). In 1868, only Hood ($66) and Riley ($88) got the aid.[24]

In 1869, a drastic change took place. Ann Riley got her $96 and Elbridge Hood his $66, but John Simpson received $375 from the town, not the state. Unfortunately, the town reports over the next three years provide only a total figure for town and state aid, but the figures, $617.81, $554.46, and $497.12, reflect the total for 1869 ($537) and suggest that the same individuals received help. In 1873, only two people are listed, Ann Riley for state aid of $96 and John Simpson for town aid of $385.04. The following year is the same; Riley got her $96 from the state, and Simpson got $383 from the town.[25]

It should be emphasized that while Nahant received compensation from the state for the payments to Ann Riley, they recovered nothing from the generous sums being paid to Simpson. Even more telling is the report for the fiscal year ending February 1877. The economic

23. Census Reports for 1860 and 1865, NHS.

24. *Annual Report for the Town of Nahant*, 1867, 1868, 1869.

25. *Annual Report for the Town of Nahant*, 1870–76.

depression that had begun in 1873 had reached its peak by 1876. As the Nahant *Annual Town Report* stated, "the paramount question in this matter [a town budget] has been to us that of economy. To refer to the general depression and prostration of business throughout the country, and to the losses and privations which all of us have thereby endured, would be needless." Of particular concern was the attempt by Boston to force Nahant's wealthy summer people to pay their taxes in the city. The report reveals deep apprehension for the financial well-being of the town. Yet, that year Nahant increased its payments to John Simpson to $525.40.[26]

Only in the report of February 1878 do we get specifics on what this money was for. The previous fiscal year, the town had given Simpson $518 for "board, hospital bills, medical attendants, etc." The following year, Simpson received $463 from the town. At the same time, Ann Riley's state aid was reduced from $96 to $48.

Ann's life reflected the typical existence of an Irish immigrant woman. In 1870, her occupation was listed as "House Keeper." The census report of 1880 reveals more and explains the reduction in state aid. By then, Ann is listed as a "Washerwoman." The number of months she was employed during the census year was eight. The categories "cannot read" and "cannot write" were both checked. Mary is no longer listed with the family, apparently having moved on with her life. Maggie is listed as eighteen years old and a "domestic servant." Therefore, by 1878, Mary had grown and left home, and Maggie was probably already working as a domestic servant. The state paid widows with children $8 a month and widows alone $4 a month; therefore, Ann's compensation was cut in half, and it would stay at $48 for the rest of her life.[27]

The Nahant aid records are pretty consistent through 1885. Ann Riley received her $48 from the state, and John Simpson averaged $366

---

26. *Annual Report for the Town of Nahant*, 1877.

27. *Annual Report for the Town of Nahant*, 1879; Census for 1880, NHS; Office of Commissioners of State Aid Returns, "Civil War Veterans' Widows: Ann Riley" file, Nahant Historical Society.

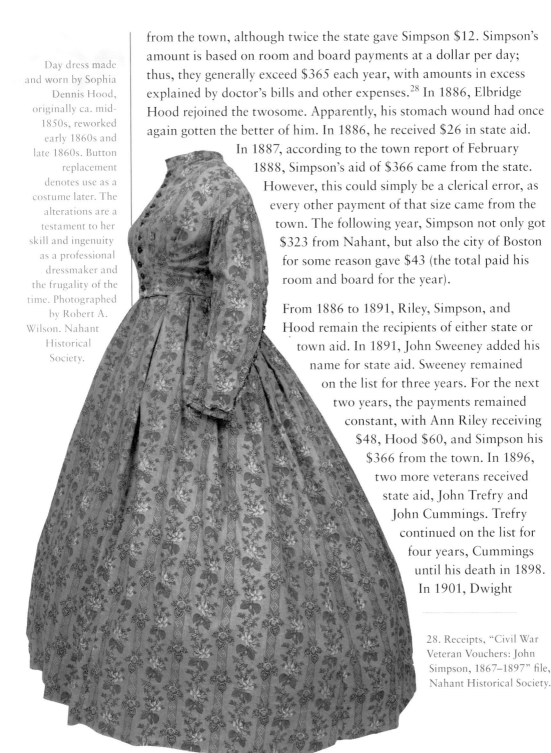

Day dress made and worn by Sophia Dennis Hood, originally ca. mid-1850s, reworked early 1860s and late 1860s. Button replacement denotes use as a costume later. The alterations are a testament to her skill and ingenuity as a professional dressmaker and the frugality of the time. Photographed by Robert A. Wilson. Nahant Historical Society.

from the town, although twice the state gave Simpson $12. Simpson's amount is based on room and board payments at a dollar per day; thus, they generally exceed $365 each year, with amounts in excess explained by doctor's bills and other expenses.[28] In 1886, Elbridge Hood rejoined the twosome. Apparently, his stomach wound had once again gotten the better of him. In 1886, he received $26 in state aid.

In 1887, according to the town report of February 1888, Simpson's aid of $366 came from the state. However, this could simply be a clerical error, as every other payment of that size came from the town. The following year, Simpson not only got $323 from Nahant, but also the city of Boston for some reason gave $43 (the total paid his room and board for the year).

From 1886 to 1891, Riley, Simpson, and Hood remain the recipients of either state or town aid. In 1891, John Sweeney added his name for state aid. Sweeney remained on the list for three years. For the next two years, the payments remained constant, with Ann Riley receiving $48, Hood $60, and Simpson his $366 from the town. In 1896, two more veterans received state aid, John Trefry and John Cummings. Trefry continued on the list for four years, Cummings until his death in 1898. In 1901, Dwight

28. Receipts, "Civil War Veteran Vouchers: John Simpson, 1867–1897" file, Nahant Historical Society.

Lamphear began to receive state aid and continued to do so at least through 1905. At that point, the town reports simply list the totals for state aid, not the specific recipients.[29]

Elbridge Hood died in 1902. He left very little for his wife, Sophia, and she had to apply to the state for a widow's pension. In doing this, Sophia was thrust into the awful paperwork hell created by the Civil War pension system. Elbridge died in early January, and by January 31, Sophia had submitted her "Declaration for a Widow's Pension."[30] On September 26, Sophia submitted an "affidavit" describing her circumstances. She owned half a house built by her husband's grandfather, and her husband's aunt owned and occupied the other half. There was a small house in the rear "not rentable" and a stable, which was being rented for "$300.00 per annum on a lease which expires next year." Sophia indicated the "rent from the stable is all the income I have except my own labor, there was no life insurance and no one is legally bound for my support."[31] The state wanted clarification, and Sophia had to submit yet another affidavit in December 1902. She indicated, "my aunt does not own any part of the stable referred to," and she said the "house is very old, one of the first built in the town."[32] It was the time before Social Security and the concept that the government is responsible for the elderly; the prospects for widows could be very bleak indeed, especially the widow of a veteran who had spent much of life suffering from a severe wound and receiving a pension. However, the government provided a widow's pension for Sophia until her death in 1913.[33]

29. *Annual Report for the Town of Nahant*, 1880–1906.

30. Declaration for a Widow's Pension, Sophia Hood, January 31, 1902. "Elbridge and Sophia Hood" file, Nahant Historical Society.

31. General Affidavitt [*sic*] for Sophia Hood, September 26, 1902. "Elbridge and Sophia Hood" file, Nahant Historical Society.

32. Affidavitt [*sic*] for Sophia Hood, December 19, 1902. "Elbridge and Sophia Hood" file, Nahant Historical Society.

33. Pensioner Dropped, Department of the Interior, Feb. 25, 1913. "Elbridge and Sophia Hood" file, Nahant Historical Society.

Eighteen ninety-seven produced significant changes in the stories of Ann Riley and John Simpson. It is quite obvious from the records that in 1897 Ann Riley had a medical crisis, which greatly reduced her ability to provide for herself. In addition to the $48 state aid, the town report reveals payments for Ann Riley at the Lynn City Hospital ($10) and $2.50 for "elastic stockings." J. C. White, a grocer, was paid $106.34 for supplying several people, including Ann Riley. In the following years, the town paid more and more for Ann. She still received her $48 from the state, but in 1898, the town provided coal, which came from Welcome Johnson. In 1899, they paid J. C. White $57.45 for food supplied to Ann and also paid for coal. Until 1907, Nahant paid J. C. White anywhere from $72 to $106 for Ann's "provisions" and between $25 and $37 for coal.

The year 1907 brought the final crisis. The *Annual Town Report* for February 1908 lists the following items: "Johnson for Riley—$11.50"; "Lawrence Cusick [a doctor and the son of Civil War veteran Thomas Cusick] for Ann Riley—$6"; "J.C. White for Ann Riley—$61.31"; and "Little Sisters of the Poor, Ann Riley—$100." The Little Sisters of the Poor was a Catholic charitable order in Lynn. It seems likely that Ann, failing in health, was sent to the Sisters to comfort her in her death.[34]

Simpson's aid from the town in 1897 was just $20, plus a "chair from Paine Furniture" for $7.50. Simpson had been moved to the Soldiers' Home in Massachusetts around that time. From that time on, there would be drastic reductions in Simpson's aid. In 1898, he was given $1.55 for supplies, and the town reimbursed T. F. Galvin for giving Simpson $5. In 1899, Nahant paid Mary Butterman $18 for boarding Simpson.

The year 1899 brought a real crisis for John Simpson and the town of Nahant, a crisis that showed the real heart of the town. It is quite evident from the records that John Simpson had become a despondent, disagreeable old man. It is easy to see that a life gone astray because of a war to preserve a country that was not even his by birthright brought this Scottish immigrant to a low level by the turn of the century. Living off the generosity of Nahant, suffering with debilitating injuries and illness, had resulted in a feeling of powerlessness, which in turn created a deep bitterness. Put simply, by 1899, no one wanted to be around this grumpy old man, and the Nahant town officers had trouble finding a place for him. Certainly, the Soldiers' Home in Massachusetts didn't want him anymore. The only alternative seemed to be the Disabled Veterans Home in Togus, Maine.[35] However, the first application to move Simpson there was disapproved in the spring of 1899.[36]

By the fall of 1899, the Soldiers' Home wanted Simpson out. On October 16, Superintendent George W. Creasy wrote to Joseph Wilson, chair of the Nahant selectmen, "Mr. John Simpson . . . has been conducting himself in such a manner that it is impossible for us to keep him longer at the home. Will you kindly arrange for his removal.[sic]"[37] In December, the president of the Soldiers' Home Board of Trustees, John G. B. Adams, wrote to Wilson, "Simpson is simply unbearable, and must be removed from the Home. He insults everyone in the Hospital, makes false statements to those who visit the Home, and in every way creates trouble." The reason why the Soldiers' Home did not toss him out on his ear, and why Simpson had become an even greater burden to Nahant, is explained in the next paragraph of the letter. Adams indicated that "were he able to walk we should be obliged to discharge him at once."[38]

A few days later, Adams wrote to Wilson again. Simpson had been examined by a doctor to determine his mental capabilities, and Adams

34. *Annual Report for the Town of Nahant*, 1898–1908.

35. Togus was the first veterans home established after the Civil War. Togus remains today a place where veterans are sent who can no longer care for themselves, and their cemetery is a miniature of Arlington National Cemetery.

36. Letter to Joseph Wilson from George W. Creasy, Superintendent of the Soldiers' Home in Massachusetts, May 12, 1899. "Civil War Veteran: John Simpson" file, Nahant Historical Society.

37. Letter to Joseph Wilson from George W. Creasy, Superintendent of the Soldiers' Home in Massachusetts, Oct. 16, 1899. "Civil War Veteran: John Simpson" file, Nahant Historical Society.

38. Letter to Joseph Wilson from John G. B. Adams, President of the Board of Trustees of the Soldiers' Home in Massachusetts, Dec. 26, 1899. "Civil War Veteran: John Simpson" file, Nahant Historical Society.

Photograph, ca. late 1800s. This home of Sophia and Elbridge Hood, now 368 Nahant Road, was a double house with the right side built first in the Federal style by 1818 and then enlarged and altered in the Greek Revival style in the mid-1800s. Hood family descendants occupied the house until 1947. It has recently been renovated into a single family home. Nahant Historical Society.

admitted "under some circumstances he would be considered insane, the Doctor says he is not, only extremely disagreeable."[39] Simpson appears to have wanted an operation, and he claimed the Soldiers' Home would not provide it. The only solution seemed to be the Disabled Veterans Home in Togus, Maine. But even there, Adams had a problem. As he wrote to Joseph Wilson on March 29, 1900, "I have never had any trouble with the people at Togus and if it was not for my friendship for you, should hesitate to inflict them with Simpson." Simpson must have been a real trial for the Soldiers' Home because Adams concluded, "I am really in doubt why such men are created but presume it is to prove to us that there is punishment before as well as after death, and am satisfied that whoever gets Simpson will have their full share."[40]

John Simpson was removed from the Soldiers' Home and brought to Nahant until he could be transferred to Togus. This meant room and board payments and transportation costs. Nahant paid Frank Phillips $85.68, Mary Butterman $80, and Charles Daily $12 for the "care and removing [of] John Simpson to Togus, Maine." The Commissioners of

State Aid compensated the town for the payments to Mary Butterman, which Commissioner Charles Hastings indicated was "about as much as this man Simpson deserves."[41]

By May 1900, Simpson was in Togus. Joseph Wilson informed the Commissioner of State Aid that support payments could be stopped (Togus was a federal hospital). The Assistant Commissioner of State Aid, Francis A. Bicknell, wrote to "thank you for the notification and to congratulate you in getting rid of him for a while at least."[42] It would be more than a while; it would be permanent. At first, Simpson seemed to like the change. He wrote to Joseph Wilson on May 23, 1900, "I am getting along very well in the hospital. The Dr says that he can perform an opperation and can make me better then I am. Will you let me know if the peopel are well and you and your family is well."[43] However, life was simply not that kind to John Simpson, and he continued in his ways. A letter written to Joseph Wilson in April 1901 from Dr. W. E. Elwell, chief surgeon at the Togus Home, is worth quoting in detail as it shows what all these people, including the people of Nahant, had to endure in the final years of John Simpson's life.

> Mr. John Simpson, who is and has been for a long time a patient in the hospital of this Home, has handed me your letter to him of the 10th inst., in which you authorize him to employ a special attendant. As I judge from this that you are not familiar with the conditions here, I have thought it best to explain just how we are situated.

39. Letter to Joseph Wilson from John G. B. Adams, President of the Board of Trustees of the Soldiers' Home in Massachusetts, Dec. 30, 1899. "Civil War Veteran: John Simpson" file, Nahant Historical Society.

40. Letter to Joseph Wilson from John G. B. Adams, President of the Board of Trustees of the Soldiers' Home in Massachusetts, March 29, 1900. "Civil War Veteran: John Simpson" file, Nahant Historical Society.

41. *Annual Report for the Town of Nahant*, 1898–1901; David M. Gosoroski, "Union Vets Lead Nation into Next Century," (*VFW*, Vol. 84, No. 9, May 1997), 29; Letter to Joseph Wilson from Commissioner of State Aid Charles W. Hastings, March 12, 1900. "Civil War Veteran: John Simpson" file, Nahant Historical Society.

Mr. Simpson, as you probably know, is a very unfortunate man, whose disabilities are so extensive and numerous that he is almost constantly uncomfortable and is also a source of great care and some annoyance to those about him. His prolonged suffering has affected his disposition and subjected him to fits of despondency which at times are of so severe a character as to indicate a failure of his mental powers. I have found it difficult to get attendants would [sic] perform the unpleasant work of properly caring for him and keeping him clean and, at the same time, stand the abuse which Mr. Simpson indulges in when under the influence of one of those melancholy attacks. I have been unable to keep him in a [sic] open ward with other patients because of their complaints in regard to his offensive language, so that I have had to provide a special room for him, and for a month had a special attendant to take care of him alone. . . . He is at times apparently cheerful, and again, so unhappy that he makes all those about him uncomfortable by his complaints and his insistence that he is going to "Leave at once and die on the first doorstep he can reach," etc., etc. He is certainly to be pitied and he has my sincere sympathy.

Elwell concluded that obtaining a "congenial companion" would be "practically impossible" because of Simpson's "disposition." Elwell recommended to Wilson that Simpson be sent "little remembrances" to "relieve the monotony and add some cheer to what must at best be a somewhat burdensome existence."[44]

The "burdensome existence" of John Simpson ended on August 14, 1904, at the Togus hospital.[45] But the story does not end there.

42. Letter to Joseph Wilson from Assistant Commissioner of State Aid Francis A Bicknell, May 4, 1900. "Civil War Veteran: John Simpson" file, Nahant Historical Society.

43. Letter to Joseph Wilson from John Simpson, May 23, 1900. "Civil War Veteran: John Simpson" file, Nahant Historical Society.

44. Letter to Joseph Wilson from Dr. W. E. Elwell, April 15, 1901. "Civil War Veteran: John Simpson" file, Nahant Historical Society.

Apparently, the town of Nahant had Simpson's body transported back to Nahant to be buried in Greenlawn Cemetery. We can only say "apparently" because there is information that Simpson is buried in Greenlawn without a headstone, that funeral expenses were paid, and that he is not buried at Togus.[46] Joseph Wilson kept Simpson's pension money and, after paying for the funeral, used the remaining money to purchase a revolving leaf exhibition rack for the Nahant Public Library. A bronze plate on the rack remembers John Simpson.[47]

I have gone into some detail in the story of Ann Riley and John Simpson for two reasons. First, these are only two people, yet the figures are impressive. The state of Massachusetts provided $2,500 for Ann Riley, and the town of Nahant about $1,300. Excluding the small amounts given by the state and the money spent on John Simpson at Togus by the federal government, Nahant alone spent $11,000 to support him. These two extreme cases for Nahant do not include Elbridge Hood, Dwight Lamphear, John Cummings, and the rest who received money. Multiply this by the hundreds of thousands of wounded veterans, widows, and orphans left after the war (one figure places the number of widows and orphans alone at 116,450), and remember that this aid lasted into the twentieth century, and one sees that the Civil War remained very much in the consciousness of American society.[48]

The second point concerns the town of Nahant itself. After all, who were Ann Riley and John Simpson? Ann and Patrick Riley were Irish immigrants who had probably not lived in Nahant long before the war began, and they arrived at a time when the Irish were not well accepted, particularly by the upper crust of Boston society who

45. Letter to Frank G. Phillips from Dr. W. E. Elwell, September 30, 1904. "Civil War Veteran: John Simpson" file, Nahant Historical Society.

46. List of Civil War Veterans buried in Greenlawn Cemetery by Phillip Applin. Nahant Historical Society; Interview with Darryl Moody, Records Office, Togus Veterans Hospital, June 12, 2006.

47. Wilson Diary, p. 4. Nahant Historical Society. The revolving rack is still at the Nahant Public Library.

48. Gosoroski, "Union Vets Lead Nation," (*VFW*, May 1997), 29.

frequented Nahant. Despite all that, Patrick Riley, like thousands of other Irish immigrants, had enlisted in an Irish regiment to help preserve his new country, and he had paid the ultimate price. A rebel bullet in a wild thunderstorm in Chantilly, Virginia, had shattered Ann Riley's dreams of the future. She was now the responsibility of the Anglo-Protestant town where her husband had left her. Nahanters did not fail her. They dutifully ensured that she received her state aid, and in her last years, when she could no longer supplement that, the veterans, and the sons of veterans, provided for her needs.

Remember that John Simpson was not even a resident of the town when he went to war. A Scottish immigrant, he had simply filled a slot to enable the town to fulfill its recruit quota. But when he became disabled, Simpson apparently had nowhere to turn. Nahant offered him a home. He had put his life on the line to help Nahant, and the citizens of Nahant, veterans and nonveterans alike, agreed to care for him, apparently when no one else would. They cared for him even during a depression and financial crisis. They paid $11,000 over three and a half decades, and yet there is no evidence of any animosity, no questions. They cared for him when he turned into a bitter, extremely unpleasant man rejected by caregivers used to dealing with unpleasant circumstances. Yet, the veterans and the people of Nahant never gave up on him. The town history simply remembers him as the man "whom people will remember limping about with a cane on account of a war injury."[49] Even more revealing is the *Annual Town Report* of February 1905 that relates Simpson's death at Togus. In the report he is referred to as "our veteran." Simpson was a veteran crushed by his war experience, a life destroyed yet still living, and the veterans and people of Nahant understood that. He belonged to the people of the town; he was their project and their responsibility.[50]

The veterans who returned to Nahant or moved there after never really left the Civil War behind. It was part of their being and part of their view of the world. They were men who had sacrificed for honor and for their country, and they were defined by their experience. These are concepts that may sound strange in our world today but not to people in the late nineteenth century. And as these veterans moved up in their world, they never forgot. Thus, for the veterans sitting on the Board of Selectmen of Nahant, using their power to help the victims of the Civil War like Ann Riley and John Simpson came very easily.

49. Wilson, *Annals*, 105.

50. *Annual Report for the Town of Nahant*, 1905.

six &

REMEMBRANCE

IN THE YEARS THAT FOLLOWED THE CIVIL WAR, THE VETERANS of that conflict kept the memory of their experience alive in many ways. The Nahant men were no different. One common method was the erection of a monument. By the end of the nineteenth century, the erection and dedication of monuments exploded across the landscape. Many of the monuments are drearily familiar, a ubiquitous granite soldier with mustache and musket held before him. Nahant avoided this duplication by erecting their monument very early. The *Annual Town Report* for February 1867 indicates an allocation of $575 for a soldier's monument in 1866.[1] The monument was placed in Greenlawn Cemetery. On it was carved the names of those who died in the war.

Although important, monuments go from dedication to familiar object to ignored. Civil War veterans sought to keep their memories alive, and continue the sense of brotherhood that military experience so often fosters, by forming various associations where they could meet, maintain their friendships, and reminisce. Nahant veterans participated in three such organizations: the Grand Army of the Republic, the Forty-fifth Massachusetts Regiment Association, and the Nahant Veterans Association.

The Grand Army of the Republic (GAR) was formed in Illinois in 1867. The fifth post established was at Lynn (General Lander Post No. 5). By the 1890s, Post No. 5 was the largest GAR post in the country.

Photograph, ca. 2006. An interior view of General Lander Post No. 5's Grand Army of the Republic Hall on Andrew Street in Lynn, Massachusetts, built 1885, deeded by special act of the Massachusetts legislature in 1919 to the city of Lynn. The post was deliberately disbanded in May 13, 1945, upon the death of its last surviving member. Over twelve hundred photographs of its members from Nahant and Lynn adorn its walls. Photographed by Robert A. Wilson. Courtesy of Grand Army of the Republic Museum, Lynn, MA.

The earliest Nahant-connected member to join was postwar resident Thomas Tibbets in 1871. Most Nahant veterans joined in the 1880s. Of the eighteen who joined the GAR Post No. 5, fourteen joined in that decade (six in 1881 alone). Some did not join until late in life. Welcome Johnson waited until 1896, Dwight Lamphear until 1904, and Edmund Johnson until 1906. They all met in a beautiful hall in Lynn, elaborately decorated and set up similarly to a Masonic temple, a fraternal order, which the GAR resembled. The large room had an altar in the center (Post No. 5 had the capstan from the *Kearsarge*), chairs for the officers in the center of each wall, and benches for the other members, all furnished with plush fabrics and carpeting typical of late Victorian interior design. At one time, George Neal, one of the Lynn men credited to Nahant during the war, served as the commander of Post No. 5.[2] The GAR held reunions as well. One of the more unusual held at East Point in Nahant in July 1887 brought together Union and Confederate veterans.[3] Women also had an outlet in the Woman's Relief Corps, GAR Auxiliary.[4]

The principles of the GAR were fraternity, charity, and loyalty. On a grand scale, the members of the GAR promoted relief for disabled and indigent veterans, a correct portrayal of the war, and nationalism. Initially, they focused on creating state homes for veterans, remembering the men who had died, and caring for the widows and orphans. We can easily see the care for John Simpson and Ann Riley coming out of this philosophy. The GAR had committees to promote historically correct textbooks for children and to oversee the teaching of the war in the classroom. It became an advocate for veterans' rights, particularly in the area of pensions, and wielded some political power, mostly for Republican administrations. At its height, it had over 425,000 members (33 percent of eligible Union veterans) and 6,928

1. *Annual Report for the Town of Nahant*, 1867.

2. Gosoroski, "Union Vets Lead Nation" (*VFW*, May 1997), 27.

3. "Nahant: Civil War Veterans" file, NHS.

4. The Nahant Historical Society owns a badge from this organization.

5. Gosoroski, "Union Vets Lead Nation" (*VFW*, May 1997), 24–30.

6. Mann, *History of the Forty-fifth*, 452, 459, 462.

posts. The GAR resisted the temptation to add Spanish-American War veterans to its ranks. Its purpose was to remember the Civil War and no other conflict, and the members designed their organization to perish with its last member (who died in 1956).[5]

A second outlet for some of the veterans from Nahant was the Forty-fifth Massachusetts Regimental Association. In fact, the Johnsons were instrumental in putting it together. Edward J. Johnson helped organize the reunions, especially the first, which took place at Whitney's Hotel on Nahant Road on September 5, 1876. Hervey Shepard Johnson served as chaplain, and Luther S. Johnson served a term as president. Not only did they hold annual reunions, they also put together a history of the regiment and, in 1891, formed the "Sons and Daughters of the Forty-fifth" to ensure that the legacy continued.[6]

But perhaps no organization meant as much to these men as the town organization, the Nahant Veterans Association. The exact date when this group formed is unknown, but it came into its own in 1894. The focus of the organization was Decoration or Memorial Day. The GAR took a special interest in Decoration Day, the "sacred festival of our dead." Although Decoration Day was observed right after the war in

Photograph, A Blue and Gray Reunion of veterans and their families from both North and South hosted by the GAR Post No. 5 at the estate of Senator Henry Cabot Lodge on East Point, Nahant, in July 1887. Courtesy of Lynn Museum and Historical Society.

many local communities, New York became the first state to proclaim May 30 as a state holiday in 1873. By 1891, all northern states had voted for the holiday.[7] The first reference in Nahant is for 1879 when the town gave $75 to Edmund B. Johnson for "Decoration Day" (the title was used interchangeably with Memorial Day until after World War I). The money figure, $75, remained pretty constant, given to Johnson, George Kibbey, or Thomas Cusick until 1894.[8]

The Nahant Veterans Association was in full control of the celebration by that point, and that year turned out to be particularly special. But who belonged to this group? Their organizational journal lists the following as members: Patrick Henry Winn, Edward J. Johnson, Edmund B. Johnson, Elbridge G. Hood, Welcome J. Johnson, Robert L. Cochrane, H. Shepard Johnson, Alfred A. Barnes, George W. Kibbey, Sidney C. Johnson, Lorenzo P. Whitney, Arthur J. Bulfinch, Edwin W. Johnson, Thomas W. Tibbets, Thomas J. Cusick, and William H. Hildreth.[9] There is no date for the list, and other names also became connected to the Nahant Veterans, including Charles Babb, James Timmins, Charles Ladd, and Baldwin Brown.[10]

Hildreth? Ladd? Brown? The answer to the question who belonged to the Nahant Veterans Association introduces us to three more men connected to the town by way of the Civil War. Charles H. Ladd was not a resident of Nahant at the time of the Civil War, nor was he credited to the town. He was born in Maine in 1846 and, at the time the war broke out, was working as a farmer in Andover, Massachusetts. On September 17, he enlisted in Company F, Forty-fifth Massachusetts Militia, the same day, company, and regiment as the Nahant Johnsons. He served with the Forty-fifth in New Bern until mustered out in July 1863. Ladd then moved to Springfield where he worked as a mechanic, possibly at the Springfield Armory. On December 31, 1863, he enlisted in Company I, Third Massachusetts

---

7. Gosoroski, "Union Vets Lead Nation" (*VFW*, May 1997), 29.

8. *Annual Report for the Town of Nahant*, 1880–94.

9. Nahant Veterans' Book, NHS, 346.

10. "Soldier Bio" file, NHS.

Photograph, Edmund B. Johnson, ca. 1885. Photographer: William Wires, New Ocean Street, Lynn, MA. Courtesy of Grand Army of the Republic Museum, Lynn, MA.

Heavy Artillery. Company I of the Third was unusual in that it consisted largely of mechanics from the Springfield Armory. Because of their special skills, Company I was detached from the regiment and assigned to the U.S. Engineers where they became experts on pontoon bridges. Ladd did well in the unit. He was promoted to first sergeant on February 10, 1864, wounded in May during the Wilderness campaign, and promoted to second lieutenant the following January. He mustered out of the service in September 1865. There

is no indication that he ever lived in Nahant after the war although
he may have been a summer resident. The Forty-fifth Massachusetts
regimental history lists him as living in Springfield in 1908, and he
was buried in Haverhill. Yet Ladd participated in the 1894 Nahant
celebrations. Obviously, his connection comes through Company F
of the Forty-fifth where he probably befriended the Nahant men and
later belonged to the Forty-fifth Regimental Association. But beyond
friendship, nothing has turned up directly tying Ladd to Nahant,
except that he was considered part of the Nahant Veterans.[11]

The same could be said for William Hildreth. He was born in Beverly,
Massachusetts, and at the age of seventeen enlisted in the Fifth
Massachusetts Militia on August 15, 1862. He served with the Fifth
at New Bern until mustered out in July 1863. Hildreth served with
the Fifth again for one-hundred-day service in 1864, mustering out as
a sergeant. After the war, he remained in the Fifth Militia, becoming
captain of the Peabody Company, and joined Post 50 of the GAR in
Peabody. Hildreth's link to Nahant seems even more tenuous than
Ladd's. The only other members of the Fifth Massachusetts associated

11. "Soldier Bio" file, NHS; *Mass. Soldiers*, 3rd Mass. Hvy. Art.; Mann, *History of the Forty-fifth*.

12. "Soldier Bio" file, NHS.

13. Photo of Baldwin Brown, Nahant Library.

with Nahant were William Gibbs, who served in a different company, and Edwin Whitney, who happened to be buried in Nahant after he died at New Bern. Yet, Hildreth was listed in the Nahant Veterans' Book, participated in the events of 1894, and even led the parade that year. Despite the strong Peabody connection, it appears Hildreth did live in Nahant or at least was a well-known summer resident.[12]

The third name associated with the Nahant Veterans is even more mysterious. Baldwin Brown apparently served in a New York regiment during the war. His name does not appear on any census for Nahant, he is not listed in the Nahant Veterans' Book, nor did he take part in the 1894 ceremonies. Yet his picture is at the town library with a notation that he belonged to the Nahant Veterans. How, why, and when may remain a mystery forever.[13]

Carte de visite, Baldwin Brown, ca. November 1862. Brown was considered a comrade in arms by the Nahant Veterans but served with a New York regiment. Photographer: Thomas H. Martin of 82 Chatham Street, New York City. Courtesy of Nahant Public Library.

All that these veterans wanted, all the philosophy behind commemorative organizations, the GAR, the Forty-fifth Massachusetts, and the Nahant Veterans, came to a pinnacle in 1894. In March at the annual town meeting, the Nahant Veterans recommended Patrick Winn, Edward J. Johnson, and William Hildreth to serve as the Memorial Day Committee. The town in turn voted $225 for the celebration, a significant increase over past years. The committee met twice in April to plan the festivities. Invitations would be sent to all veterans in town, the School Committee for all the school children, and GAR Post 5. "Also that Comrade E. J. Johnson be detailed to address the scholars of the public schools on his experience in the late Civil War."[14]

Then in mid-May, the Nahant Veterans received a gift from one of their own. Luther S. Johnson, now a manufacturer in Lynn, sent the Nahant Veterans a flag and a letter of explanation.

Lynn, May 19, 1894

To Mr. E.J. Johnson,

Standard Bearer of the Nahant Veterans

DEAR SIR: It gives me great pleasure to have the opportunity of presenting this flag to your organization, "The Nahant Veterans," and may it be your pride and ambition in the future, as in the past, to uphold and protect what it symbolizes—loyalty, justice and freedom to every American citizen.

Accept my thanks, and believe me one of your loyal organization.

I am sincerely yours,

Luther S. Johnson[15]

Edward J. Johnson's GAR membership badges, ca. 1885. Both the National GAR badge (left) and the Massachusetts state GAR badge (right) are shown here. Courtesy of Nahant Public Library.

Such a gift needed an appropriate response, and so the Nahant Veterans met on May 22 to formulate one. "A suitable letter in reply was read, also an indenture which was signed by Nahant Veterans."[16] The letter of thanks said:

Nahant, Mass., Tuesday, May 22, 1894

To Luther S. Johnson, Esq.,

Dear Comrade: At a meeting of the Nahant Veterans held at Nahant, your letter presenting the beautiful silk flag was read. This gift comes very near our hearts, as you have shared with us the march and camp, the whirl and storm of battle. None but a soldier can know what this flag means to you and us. We need not, by word or resolve, express our gratitude and thanks, for in our hearts we will ever hold dear this flag.

With grateful memories of you as comrade and donor, and in acknowledgment of this gift, we all subscribe our names.

Patrick Henry Winn
Edward J. Johnson

Edward J. Johnson, ca. 1885. Photographer: William Wires, New Ocean Street, Lynn, MA. Courtesy of Grand Army of the Republic Museum, Lynn, MA.

14. *Annual Report for the Town of Nahant*, 1895; Nahant Veterans' Book, NHS, 11–13.

15. "Town of Nahant Memorial Day 1894" (Pamphlet, NHS).

16. Nahant Veterans' Book, NHS, 15.

William H. Hildreth
Edmund B. Johnson
Elbridge G. Hood
Welcome J. Johnson
Robert L. Cochrane
H. Shepard Johnson
Alfred A. Barnes
George W. Kibbey
Sidney C. Johnson
L. P. Whitney
Arthur J. Bulfinch
Edwin W. Johnson
Charles H. Ladd
Charles N. Babb

Not only did they thank Luther Johnson, they made a solemn pledge concerning the flag.

Indenture of the Nahant Veterans

Be it Remembered, that we, Edward J. Johnson, R. L. Cochrane and A. A. Barnes, in whose custody the care and keeping of this flag is now placed, do faithfully promise that we will guard and keep it, until the same shall be placed in the niche to be provided for it, in the new library building now being built, and that we will place the same in the hands of our successors, who may be appointed by the Nahant Veterans.

Edward J. Johnson
Robert L. Cochrane
Alfred A. Barnes

And further, we, the Nahant Veterans, agree, vote and declare that the last survivors, or survivor, shall surrender this flag to the care and keeping of the citizens of the town of Nahant, in remembrance of its veteran soldiers and sailors of the late rebellion, by them to be kept forever. And we, the Veterans in meeting assembled, hereby subscribe our names in the presence of each other to the

above written obligation, and until then, this obligation will be kept in faithful remembrance by us.

Patrick Henry Winn
Edward J. Johnson
William H. Hildreth
Edmund B. Johnson
Elbridge G. Hood
Welcome J. Johnson
Robert L. Cochrane
H. Shepard Johnson
Alfred A. Barnes
Luther S. Johnson
George W. Kibbey
Sidney C. Johnson
L. P. Whitney
Arthur J. Bulfinch
Edwin W. Johnson
Charles H. Ladd
Charles N. Babb

After this, according to the minutes, "the Chairman of the Committee P.H. Winn in a very patriotic address then presented the flag to the color guard—E.J. Johnson, Sergeant, R. Cochrane, Corp. of Guard, A. A. Barnes, Corp. of Guard."[17]

The $225 from the town was duly spent on supplies for the coming celebration. Among the items purchased were four hundred rolls and six loaves of bread from a baker and from the grocer J. C. White, forty-two pounds of "cow tongue," fifty-seven pounds of ham, sixteen pounds of "java coffee," twenty-five pounds of sugar, and six "mugs" of mustard. Other expenses included engaging a band for $75, hiring a caterer, paying a printer for the programs, and purchasing one hundred small flags for decoration, twenty-five yards of white paper, and "two boxes cigars."[18]

According to the Nahant Veterans secretary, Edward J. Johnson, May 30, "after the two previous days of storms and rain, came with sunshine and west wind. All work in this town was laid aside, the citizens devoting this day in a patriotic manner to the memory of its citizen soldiers, who served in the war to preserve the union of the United States, and who are now buried in Greenlawn Cemetery." The procession included police, the Salem Cadet Band, the Nahant Fire Department, the town selectmen, School Committee, a detachment from GAR Post 5, the Nahant Veterans, and the "School Battalion" commanded by Elbridge Hood.[19]

At the cemetery, Jonathan E. Johnson delivered an address that caught not only the spirit of the day but also the hopes and desires of all the Nahant Veterans. He addressed the reasons why they had gone to war and dispelled any lingering thoughts that they went to war for pecuniary gain.

> In the '60's the great body of our young fellows went. There was enthusiasm, tremendous, heartrending enthusiasm. But there followed the severe weeks of drill . . . the months and years of hard, man-killing campaigning through mud or dust or sand, in the swamps and the woods, under the pouring rain or the scorching southern suns, in weariness and in sickness—the awful danger and shock of battle—the irksome monotony of camp life, with drill and drill and drill—perhaps also the long starvation of rebel prisons. These things our soldiers accomplished, not in long bursts of excitement, not in thrilling moments of enthusiasm— rather in homesickness, in weariness, in discomfort. They did it by force of cool determination—of gritty, dogged resoluteness. And deep down beneath the surface, I believe under all the joking and swearing and roughness and happy-go-luckiness of it all, they did

Luther Scott Johnson, ca. 1885. Photographer: William Wires, New Ocean Street, Lynn, MA. Courtesy of Grand Army of the Republic Museum, Lynn, MA.

17. "Town of Nahant Memorial Day 1894" (Pamphlet, NHS); Nahant Veterans' Book, NHS, 15.

18. Nahant Veterans' Book, NHS, 17–19.

19. Nahant Veterans' Book, NHS, 21–23.

Opposite page: Patrick Lenehan's GAR uniform, ca. 1885, 20 oz. dark navy wool with bright brass buttons. Nahant Veterans wore this when they attended meetings at General Lander GAR Post No. 5 in Lynn, Massachusetts, or at the various encampments held elsewhere. Photograph by Robert A. Wilson. Nahant Historical Society.

This page: Patrick Lenehan's GAR badges, ca. 1885–1917. In addition to the national GAR badge with the bronze star and flag stripe ribbon, the other three are encampment badges from attending GAR reunion encampments. Nahant Historical Society.

it by the consecrating power of an ever-growing love for this land of ours, in the conviction that it was all worthwhile, if only the nation was saved, and the old flag carried back with honor and preserved for them and their children. It took more than excitement to finish that war—it took discipline and love and self-sacrifice.

Again, some might say that the motives of our soldiers were mercenary. They enlisted to get government money, bounties and pensions. As regards government money, the government paid $13 a month per man. I don't believe that there was a man in this town that enlisted that could not earn at least six times that amount, at his own business in his own home. In most cases, I fancy these few paltry dollars were kept for pocket money, or sent to the family at home. As regards bounties, the towns paid one or two hundred dollars per man, and generous individuals may have contributed more. But this was no compensation for the soldier. It is absurd to suppose it—it was merely the natural recognition as far as could be made, of priceless public duty performed. No man in his senses would run the risk of sudden death, wasting disease, or starvation-imprisonment for that. But there were bounty-jumpers you may say. Yes, there were. This world is so made by God that wherever there is a possibility of good, there must be possibility for evil also. The very condition and chance of being good is also the condition of the possibility of being evil. In the acre of this world must be sown not only good seeds but also the tares and the weeds, and they must grow together until the harvest. So there were bounty-jumpers and sneaks in our army—but, thank God, they were not the typical soldiers of that army. Sherman would never have made his splendid march, or Grant never have fought out that fearful campaign through the wilderness to Petersburg if they had been. Those young fellows in blue were in earnest—they weren't out there in that sort of business to make money—they were the best young blood of this nation, dying by the thousands and suffering every man of them for our good and for the nation's good.

No, as far as I can see, the enlistment of our soldiers in that war was an act of sacrifice and heroism. The body of those that went were young fellows. They had learned their trades, started in business, begun the practice of their professions, were graduating from our colleges. They had prospects, just as we young men to-day have our prospects. They were at work, at home among their own people, and content. They left this for what? For drill, army discipline, killing, physical exposure, strong probability of suffering by disease or wounds, for the prospect of sudden and

violent death far from home. They gave up business prospects, the ambitions of their life, home, and the loved ones there, even life, if need should be. If this was not sacrifice, sacrifice of self, then, I for my part, don't know what self-sacrifice is. What was the motive of this sacrifice and devotion? Our country—the nation. How worthy they must have thought her, how fair

Elbridge G. Hood, ca. 1885. Photographer: William Wires, New Ocean Street, Lynn, MA. Courtesy of Grand Army of the Republic Museum, Lynn, MA.

MEMORIAL POEM.

This poem was written by Mrs. ANNIE E. JOHNSON, and was read by
Mr. FRED A. WILSON, Memorial Day, 1894.

MEMORIAL DAY.

Children, with wreaths of flowers,
  Wait in the quiet street,
Where, under the arching elm-trees
  We can see the soldiers meet.

The boys in blue of the Army!
  Beneath this sky of May,
Ye come, bringing many a memory
  To hallow Memorial Day.

Now beneath their starry banner
  Once more have the soldiers met—
Where your fallen comrades are lying
  Oh, brothers! ye do not forget!

As they march away, shoulder to shoulder
  We recall a sadder day,
(Though the faces are graver and older,
  And the bonnie brown locks are grey).

When one, from each kindred household,
  Went forth at the trumpet's call,
Fathers, and sons, and brothers,
  —Not a coward among them all!—

Ye of the grand old Army!
  Beneath this sky of May,
Ye bring memories, proud, and tender,
  To hallow Memorial Day!

Of the letters from lonely firesides—
  (Ah, mothers! whose hands so dear
Have fallen from our clasp,) we remember
  Your love with its hope and fear.

And we know how those letters were treasured,
  'Mid the battle's smoke and noise,
As if they were sacred amulets,
  That guarded the lives of " our boys."

By the thrill of pride and anguish
  That swept through our souls like flame,
We knew that our Country was dearest,
  And Liberty more than a name!

And thus in this beautiful May-time
  With the breeze, and the wind's light play,
Came to us the grandest lesson
  That could hallow Memorial Day!

Opposite page top: Patrick Lenehan's family home, pictured here around the last quarter of the nineteenth century, now 181 Nahant Road, was built postwar and remains in the family. His wife, Mary, is pictured with their children. Nahant Historical Society.

Bottom: Annie E. Johnson (1827–1916) was a Nahant poet, the author of *Songs from Nahant*, and a friend of Longfellow. She was the sister of Edward J. Johnson and also a painter of landscapes.

This page left: Badge, the GAR auxiliary, the Woman's Relief Corps, worn by an unknown Nahant woman, a relative of one of the Nahant Veterans This vital postwar organization did much to ameliorate the sufferings of the soldiers' families. Nahant Historical Society.

Below: Photograph, Nahant Veterans Association posing in front of the Nahant Public Library on Decoration Day 1910. Nahant Historical Society.

and glorious she must have shone before their eyes, that they were willing to give so much for her sake!

Johnson then reminded everyone that this day was to remember and honor those who did not return. He also touched on the deep feeling the veterans had for the battlefields on which they fought.

The nation is sacred to us because of the devotion and sacrifice of living. It becomes doubly sacred to us because of the blood of our dead. The soil on which their blood was poured is different from any other soil for us—it is hallowed. We thank God for them first, that our nation could nurture sons like those sons. And then we must remember, and can never forget, that their blood was shed for us and in our stead. They brought everything for us, our country, peace, prosperity and honor. Since the war we have grown enormously as a country. It all began with the war. That awful sacrifice of blood and suffering aroused the nation. A thrill of new life seemed to pulsate through its veins. With a new heart it sprang into new being into new energies, into ever renewed and ever greater action. The nation had been vindicated. It had been glorified by its sons. They had showed to the world once for all that this nation was worth more than money and property, worth more than human life itself.

Left: Patrick Lenehan, ca. 1885. Photographer: William Wires, New Ocean Street, Lynn, MA. Courtesy of Grand Army of the Republic Museum, Lynn, MA.

Right: Fred A. Trefethan, ca. 1885. Photographer: William Wires, New Ocean Street, Lynn, MA. Courtesy of Grand Army of the Republic Museum, Lynn, MA.

Finally Johnson addressed the new symbol of this war, the flag given by Luther Johnson and proudly carried by the Nahant Veterans for the first time.

We feel all this whenever we see the old flag. All that our country means to us, we feel when we see it. And surely there is something sacred, something divine there. Why do our hearts thrill at the sight of it? Something more than just what we see with our eyes is there. Is it only a piece of silk dyed red and white and blue? Oh, it is so much more to us than that! It stands for home, for our fathers, for heroism, for our dead, for our honor, for all that is holy and sacred to man. God is speaking to us through that flag. Every rustle of its dear old folds is sweet in our ears, because it is eloquent with the voice of God. It is fitting that we should take it with us into God's House. Our dead have died for it. We shall teach our children to love it. God has blessed it. His church then may receive it and consecrate it. The Church of God is the proper and natural home for our flag.

This flag here before us must ever be peculiarly sacred to our own dear town of Nahant. It belongs to our own Nahant Veterans. It represents the devotion and loyalty of our own townsmen to this nation during the war. It was given by a veteran to veterans, in memory of their common experience together in the war and in the hope, as the generous donor has written—"that it may be their pride and ambition in the future as in the past to uphold and protect what it symbolizes—loyalty, justice and freedom to every American citizen." It shall be the privilege of veterans alone to guard it and to use it. When not in use it shall be preserved in a public niche to be provided for it in the new public library

Alfred A. Barnes, ca. 1885. Photographer: William Wires, New Ocean Street, Lynn, MA. Courtesy of Grand Army of the Republic Museum, Lynn, MA.

building. But this life is mortal. We cannot live always. And when of this group of loyal men now in our presence, envious time shall have spared to us but one, it shall be his duty—in the words of the indenture drawn up by our veterans themselves—"to surrender this flag to the care and keeping of the citizens of the town of Nahant—in remembrance of its veteran soldiers and sailors of the late rebellion, by them to be kept forever." To succeeding generations it shall be a very precious public relic. Suppose we had a flag which once was carried by our townsmen as soldiers of the Revolution, how we should prize it to-day! With what pride we would guard it and speak of it now! Yet this flag shall some day be as precious to the unborn children of the future. What a noble relic for our soldier citizens to leave to their coming fellow-citizens! How fitting! How peculiarly appropriate it is, that the memento, the relic our soldiers shall leave us to preserve, shall be their flag. Mute reminder! Silent witness! How eloquently it shall plead for the cause of devotion, and loyalty to our nation. We must keep it in the same spirit with which they kept it and handed it down to

From top left:
George C. Neal, ca. 1885. Photographer: William Wires, New Ocean Street, Lynn MA. Courtesy of Grand Army of the Republic Museum, Lynn MA.

Charles Quimby, ca. 1885. Photographer: William Wires, New Ocean Street, Lynn, MA. Courtesy of Grand Army of the Republic Museum, Lynn, MA.

Robert Cochrane, ca. 1885. Photographer: William Wires, New Ocean Street, Lynn, MA. Courtesy of Grand Army of the Republic Museum, Lynn, MA

John H. Cummings, ca. 1885. Photographer: William Wires, New Ocean Street, Lynn, MA. Courtesy of Grand Army of the Republic Museum, Lynn, MA.

Thomas Cusick, ca. 1885. Photographer: William Wires, New Ocean Street, Lynn, MA. Courtesy of Grand Army of the Republic Museum, Lynn, MA.

us, stainless and with honor! We need such mementoes [*sic*] in our task of citizenship—we feel that we and the future need them—we thank God for our townsmen that they could leave us such a memento.

Truly, Johnson knew his neighbors and knew what this day meant to them and to their hope for the future. There is a consistency in the message of Civil War veterans, whether in large organizations such as the GAR or in small groups like the Nahant Veterans. They were proud of their participation in the Civil War. They had been united in a common goal to preserve their country. They wanted all Americans to remember the "good fight" they had waged and never forget the sacrifices of so many. And they wanted America to remember this the way the veterans remembered it.

To the Nahant Veterans, Memorial Day, May 30, 1894, became a point of convergence for all these cherished beliefs. Memorial Day was their day to remember their fallen comrades and to focus the attention of the town on the Civil War. And now they had the Veterans Flag, a symbol that would extend the remembrance long after they were gone. As Edward J. Johnson would record in the Nahant Veterans' Book— after the parade, the speeches, the poems, the food, the cigars, and the fireman's baseball game on the Nahant Club grounds—"so this day passed as one to be remembered by both ex-soldiers and citizens."

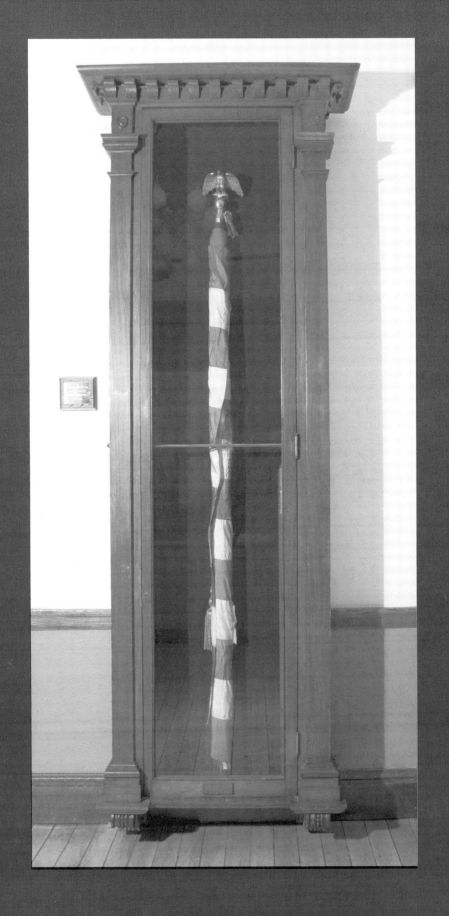

seven

PASSING ON

Of course, the work of the Nahant Veterans and the Memorial Day observances did not end in 1894. The town maintained the financial support, even increasing it to $250. The Nahant Veterans met every March to commence the planning. They picked the three-man committee and also the three-man color guard for the Veterans' Flag. The band was hired, speakers found, food and cigars purchased, and the details duly written in the Nahant Veterans' Book along with copies of the programs and newspaper clippings. In 1895, the new library was completed with a display case for the flag, there, in the words of Edward J. Johnson, "to remain forever, as a sentinel, always silently imparting its patriotic influences to the present generations and to those that are to follow."[1] As always, the meetings of the Nahant Veterans had a dual purpose: one was the important and serious duty of planning the Memorial Day celebration; and the other was social, such as on March 2, 1896, when Edward J. Johnson recorded that "after a very pleasant evening, spent in chat and good cheer, the meeting adjourned at 9:30 o'clock."[2] However, something else begins to appear in the Nahant Veterans' Book in 1899. At the meeting on February 15, E. B. Johnson made a motion requesting that E. J. Johnson "write a biography of our late member Arthur J. Bulfinch."[3] The Nahant Veterans had begun to die.

Bulfinch was the first of the Nahant Veterans Association to die, but other veterans had gone before. The first that we know of was Charles

Photograph, the 1894 Nahant Veterans Association flag and pole symbolizing "loyalty, justice and freedom" was given by Luther S. Johnson and placed in this case originally at the Nahant Public Library (built 1895), and then moved to the new Nahant Town Hall (built 1912). The widow of Luther S. Johnson replaced the original flag in 1919. All were recently conserved and moved by the Society to the Nahant Community Center, formerly the Valley Road School, in 2005. Photographer: Robert A. Wilson. Nahant Historical Society.

H. Palmer, who passed away on April 2, 1881. As Palmer had been one of the oldest to go to war at age forty-three, his early death is not surprising. Michael Mitchell died in 1886 and Albert Wilson in 1895. Eighteen ninety-eight proved the first of several difficult years. Beside Arthur Bulfinch, Charles Quimby and John Cummings died that year.[4]

By the turn of the century, it is quite evident that the Civil War generation was passing the control of the town to others. The last Civil War veteran to serve as selectman was Edwin W. Johnson in 1885. Edmund B. Johnson relinquished the office of town treasurer in 1898, and Hervey Shepard Johnson left the School Committee the following year. The last Civil War veteran to hold any kind of official office was George Kibbey, who served as highway surveyor as late as 1907.[5] Perhaps the most poignant evidence of the disappearance of these men from Nahant society is contained in the Nahant Veterans' Book. From 1894, Edward J. Johnson served as clerk and treasurer, and he dutifully recorded the minutes of the meetings and the disbursement of the town's contributions. The last minutes recorded concern the planning for Memorial Day in 1901. Edward J. Johnson was once again the clerk and treasurer. However, Edmund B. Johnson recorded the expenditures in May. Edward probably was too ill. He died on July 14. There are no more minutes recorded in the book, just a couple of letters pasted in and the death notice of Hervey Shepard Johnson, who died in 1905. Edward's hand was no longer available to keep the minutes.[6]

As the twentieth century grew older, Nahant's veterans slipped away. A few years stick out. In 1912, Edwin W. Johnson and Welcome J. Johnson died. Two years later, Edmund B. and Luther S. Johnson both passed away, as did Joseph Goode and Andrew Fuller. In terms

1. Lynn *Daily Evening Item*, May 30, 1895.

2. Nahant Veterans' Book, NHS, 37.

3. Nahant Veterans' Book, NHS, 53–54.

4. "Soldier Bio" file, NHS.

5. Wilson, *Annals*, 395–402.

6. Nahant Veterans' Book, NHS, 59, 63.

of numbers, that was the worst year, although three men died in one month in 1927 (Edward C. Johnson, Thomas Cusick, and Charles Babb), and in 1928, three more went: William Hildreth, Patrick Lenehan, and Fred Trefethan.[7]

Newspaper reports of some of the funerals show immense feeling on the part of the community. A few examples will suffice. When Hervey Shepard Johnson died in 1905, the Lynn *Daily Evening Item* wrote of his funeral and published an article on his war experiences. They described a "bier piled high with beautiful floral tributes." The Independent Church where he had served as an officer "was filled . . . with people. A quartet from Lynn rendered several beautiful selections. Following the services of the family a delegation from General Lander Post 5, GAR . . . gathered about the casket where their beautiful burial ritual was performed."[8]

In 1922, the Lynn newspaper reported that the funeral of Robert Cochrane was "attended by an unprecedentedly large number of the town's residents in recognition of the deceased's service and popularity. Post 5 GAR of Lynn and the Mortimer G. Robbins Post of the American Legion of Nahant had large delegations in attendance and participated in the services. The funeral cortege from the house to the cemetery was composed of the two veteran organizations, town officials, and a large number of friends and fellow citizens."[9] When Thomas Cusick passed away in 1927, the Lynn *Item* said, "Nahant today honored the memory of one of its leading citizens in attending the funeral of Thomas J. Cusick, former postmaster and chief of the fire department and Civil War veteran. . . . Both gray haired soldiers of the Civil War and those of the World War joined in honoring the deceased with a military funeral. . . . Services were held at the Cusick home at 165 Willow Road, Nahant . . . conducted by members of Post 5, GAR of Lynn of which the deceased was a member. . . . The house was filled with friends and relatives and there were large displays of beautiful

7. "Soldier Bio" file, NHS.

8. Lynn *Daily Evening Item*, May 16, 1905.

9. Lynn *Daily Evening Item*, April 3, 1922.

flowers. The casket was draped with the Robert L. Cochrane flag of the American Legion. . . . There was a solemn high mass at St. Thomas Aquinas Church . . . The church was filled with friends and relatives, in fact, it seemed that the whole of Nahant turned out to pay respect to the memory of this man who had given much of his life to public service."[10]

Cusick was buried at the Holyhood Cemetery in Brookline, Massachusetts, but many of the Nahant veterans were buried in the town's Greenlawn Cemetery (see Appendix). Two men became part of Nahant's Civil War history simply by being buried in that cemetery. David Nelson Lander was born in Maine and enlisted on May 15, 1863, in the Seventh Maine Volunteer Infantry. Lander probably joined the regiment in time for the Mine Run campaign in November 1863. The Seventh Maine belonged to the Sixth Corps, and in 1864, they participated in Grant's campaign against Lee, the repulse and pursuit of Jubal Early from Washington, D.C., and then with Philip Sheridan in the Shenandoah Valley campaign that fall, including the battles of Winchester, Fishers Hill, and Cedar Creek. The Sixth Corps then rejoined the lines around Petersburg and served with the Army of the Potomac until the end of the war.[11] After the war, Lander moved to Lynn and served in the city police department. He also joined GAR Post 5. He married Annette Gertrude Johnson of the original Nahant Johnsons, and thus through his wife's family, he was buried in Greenlawn Cemetery.[12]

Charles R. Whitney was connected to Nahant through the Whitney family, which included Lorenzo Whitney. Charles was born in Charlestown, Massachusetts, and was the brother of Edwin F. Whitney, who died in New Bern in 1863 and was buried in Nahant. Charles served in the Eleventh Battery, Massachusetts Light Artillery, the same unit as Charles Babb and Arthur Bulfinch. He lived in Charlestown after the war, and although he undoubtedly visited Nahant and the

10. Lynn *Daily Evening Item*, March 11, 1927.

11. *Maine at Gettysburg* (Portland, ME, 1898), 440–65.

12. "Soldier Bio" file, NHS.

Whitney family, his only Civil War connection is that he was buried in Greenlawn.[13]

Lorenzo Whitney was the last of the wartime resident veterans to die (1922). The last Civil War veteran living in town when he passed away was Patrick Lenehan. An article in the Lynn *Daily Evening Item* of April 4, 1927, reported that "Patrick Lenehan, Nahant's 82 year old Civil War veteran, will, this week, celebrate his 53rd year as a resident of Nahant, having arrived there as a young man in the early part of April 1874. For several years, Mr. Lenehan was one of three Civil War veterans in the town, but today, since the death of his two other comrades,[14] he has the distinction of being the only one in town. . . . He is an exceptionally active man for his age and enjoys being outdoors."[15] Lenehan died on June 1, 1928. According to the Lynn paper, as he lay dying in bed, Lenehan was disturbed to miss the Memorial Day services. "In order to prevent him from attempting to leave his bed he was told that the services had been postponed. So that he might not be disturbed, there was no band music in the Nahant cemetery exercises." The Lynn newspaper described him as a "Gentleman of the Old School. He was one of the finest of characters. Honest to almost a fault."[16]

Alfred A. Barnes was the last to go. Although he had moved to Lynn near the end of his life, Barnes never forgot his responsibility. He had signed the Veterans' Flag indenture and had served on the first color guard. The indenture had charged the last survivor to "surrender this flag to the care and keeping of the citizens of the town of Nahant, in remembrance of its veteran soldiers and sailors of the late rebellion, by them to be kept forever." There was even some symbolism in the history of the flag. Like the veterans themselves, the original flag wore out and had to be replaced around 1919.[17] On Memorial Day, May 30, 1929,

13. "Soldier Bio" file, NHS; Lynn *Daily Evening Item* article on December 10, 1909, stated that Whitney "was born in Charlestown and has always made his home there."

14. Thomas Cusick and Edward C. Crosby had died in March. Charles Babb died as well, but he was living in Lynn at the time.

15. Lynn *Daily Evening Item*, April 4, 1927.

16. Lynn *Daily Evening Item*, June 1, 1928.

Barnes formally turned the flag over to the American Legion and the Town of Nahant. The final duty was performed. Alfred Barnes passed away on August 7, 1934, Nahant's last direct connection to the Civil War.[18]

What can we say is the legacy of these men to Nahant? Perhaps there is the obvious legacy of descendants. Joseph Goode's descendants still run the Goode Brush Co.; Edward Crosby Johnson's descendants still summer on Nahant; Joseph Lermond is the grandson of Patrick Lenehan; and Calantha Sears, curator of the Nahant Historical Society, descends from Albert Wilson. That is only a sampling. Like all the rest of America, Nahant still celebrates Memorial Day. Unfortunately, the rolls of dead fallen in foreign wars have grown since the nineteenth century. This expansion of the holiday from a purely Civil War remembrance to embrace the dead from all American wars was accepted and encouraged by Civil War veterans after the Spanish-American War and World War I. Whether they would have accepted the holiday being moved from May 30 to create a long weekend holiday will never be known. Certainly, they approached the day with great solemnity and reverence, as befits people who experienced the bloodiest war in our history.

As for the "proper" view of the Civil War promoted by the GAR and all veterans, it does not remain quite so clean, so free of blemishes, but the important thing to them was not to forget. They certainly would have applauded the 1990 documentary by Ken Burns and appreciated the emotions triggered by that series, emotions that have led to a growing interest in Civil War history and a continued concern for the preservation of Civil War battlefields. Never forgetting, that was key. For Nahant veterans, the flag donated by Luther S. Johnson was to enfold their memories, to "remain forever, as a sentinel" to allow people to pause and reflect. It is still on display in the Nahant Historical Society. Whether it will continue to fulfill its duty, only time will tell.

17. Wilson Diary, p. 5. Nahant Historical Society. The replacement flag has forty-eight stars. Mrs. Luther Johnson paid for the replacement.

18. "Soldier Bio" file, NHS.

Opposite page: Nahant veteran Alfred A. Barnes with Nahant schoolchildren in front of the Nahant Public Library on Memorial Day, May 30, 1910. Nahant Historical Society.

NAHANT CIVIL WAR VETERANS BURIED IN GREENLAWN CEMETERY
(COMPILED BY PHILLIP APPLIN)

Charles N. Babb

Alfred A. Barnes

Arthur Bulfinch

Robert Cochrane

Frank Deshon

Elbridge G. Hood

Charles W. Johnson

Edmund B. Johnson

Edward J. Johnson

Edwin W. Johnson

Hervey Shepard Johnson

Welcome J. Johnson

David Nelson Lander

Charles Horton Palmer

John Simpson
(no stone, but a record indicates he is buried there, not in Togus)

John Trefry
(buried with no stone)

Benjamin F. Waldo

Charles R. Whitney

Edwin F. Whitney

Lorenzo P. Whitney

Albert Wilson

Secondary Sources

Ancestry.com. John H. G. Hood, Kansas Civil War Soldiers Records. http://search.ancestry.com/.

Atlas of the Town of Nahant, Massachusetts. From Official Records, Private Plans and Actual Surveys. G. M. Hopkins, C.E., 320 Walnut Street, Philadelphia, 1880.

Atlas to Accompany the Official Records of the Union and Confederate Armies. Washington, DC, 1891–1895.

Ayer, Hannah Palfry. *A Legacy of New England: Letters of the Palfry Family.* Boston, 1950.

Boynton, Charles. *The History of the Navy During the Rebellion.* New York: D. Appleton, 1867.

"Charley Longfellow Goes to War." *Harvard Library Bulletin.* Spring, 1960.

Cogswell, Leander W. *A History of the Eleventh New Hampshire Regiment Volunteer Infantry in the Rebellion War, 1861–65.* Concord, NH: Republican Press Assn., 1891.

Conyngham, D. P. *The Irish Brigade and Its Campaigns.* Boston, 1869; reprinted Gaithersburg, MD, 1987.

Current, Richard Nelson. *Lincoln's Loyalists: Union Soldiers from the Confederacy.* Boston: Northeastern University Press, 1992.

Foote, Shelby. *The Civil War, A Narrative: Fort Sumter to Perryville.* New York: Random House, 1958.

———. *The Civil War, A Narrative: Red River to Appomattox.* New York: Random House, 1974.

Gosoroski, David M. "Union Vets Lead Nation into Next Century." *VFW,* Vol. 84, No. 9, May 1997.

Hennessy, John J. *Return to Bull Run: The Campaign and Battle of Second Manassas.* New York: Simon & Schuster, 1993.

Hunter, Alvah F. *A Year on a Monitor and the Destruction of Fort Sumter* (edited and with an introduction by Craig L. Symonds). Columbia, SC: University of South Carolina Press, 1987.

Kansas Historical Society, http://www.kshs.org/genealogists/military/7thks.htm.

Keats, Susan E. *There Will Be Dancing.* Boston: FMR Corp., 2000.

Long, E. B. *The Civil War Day by Day: An Almanac, 1861–1865.* Garden City, NY: Doubleday, 1971.

Longfellow, Samuel, ed. *Life of Henry Wadsworth Longfellow with Extracts from His Journals and Correspondence.* Vol. II, 1891; reprinted New York: Greenwood Press, 1969.

Lord, Francis A. *They Fought for the Union.* New York: 1960.

Maine at Gettysburg. Portland, ME: 1898.

Mann, Albert W. *History of the Forty-fifth Regiment, Massachusetts Volunteer Militia, "The Cadet Regiment."* Boston: W. Spooner, 1908.

Massachusetts Adjutant General's Office. *Massachusetts Soldiers, Sailors and Marines in the Civil War.* Boston: Wright & Potter Printing Co., 1937.

Massey, Mary Elizabeth. *Women in the Civil War.* 1966; reprint Lincoln, NE: University of Nebraska Press, 1994.

Military medical and surgical essays; prepared for the United States Sanitary Commission, WorldCat Libraries, http://www.worldcatlibraries.org/wcpa/top3mset/32389d93b4ce48bd.html.

Paterson, Stanley C. and Carl G. Seaburg. *Nahant on the Rocks.* Nahant Historical Society, 1991.

Priest, John Michael. *Antietam: The Soldier's Battle.* Shippensburg, PA: White Mane Pub. Co., 1989.

United States Sanitary Commission: A Sketch of Its Purposes and Its Work. Boston: Little, Brown and Co., 1863.

"USS *Nahant* (1862–1904)," Naval Historical Center Website, http://www.history.navy.mil/photos/sh-usn/usnsh-n/nahant.htm.

Walker, Francis. *History of the Second Corps in the Army of the Potomac.* New York: 1887.

Wert, Jeffry D. *General James Longstreet: The Confederacy's Most Controversial Soldier—A Biography.* New York: Simon & Schuster, 1993.

Wilson, Fred A. *Some Annals of Nahant, Massachusetts.* Boston: Old Corner Book Store, 1928.

Newspapers

Lynn (MA) Daily Evening Item, May 30, 1895.

Lynn (MA) Daily Evening Item, May 16, 1905, Johnson obituary.

Lynn (MA) Daily Evening Item, February 24, 1908.

Lynn (MA) Daily Evening Item, December 10, 1909.

Lynn (MA) Daily Evening Item, July 14, 1911.

Lynn (MA) Daily Evening Item, February 15, 1913, Johnson obituary.

Lynn (MA) Daily Evening Item, April 3, 1922.

Lynn (MA) Daily Evening Item, March 11, 1927.

Lynn (MA) Daily Evening Item, April 4, 1927.

Lynn (MA) Daily Evening Item, June 1, 1928.

Lynn (MA) Daily Evening Item, December 14, 1929, Neal obituary.

Interviews

Calantha Sears, Curator, Nahant Historical Society, June 2006.

Darryl Moody, Records Office, Togus Veterans Hospital, June 12, 2006.

Primary Sources

Official Records

Annual Reports for the Town of Nahant, 1864–1908.

Census Report for 1880, Nahant Historical Society.

Census Reports for 1860 and 1865, Nahant Historical Society.

Massachusetts Adjutant General's Report for 1866. Report by W. H. Johnson, Chairman, Selectmen of Nahant.

Nahant Town Census, 1860 and 1865, Nahant Historical Society.

Ninth Annual Report of the School Committee of the Town of Nahant, February 28, 1862 (Lynn, MA, 1862).

Tenth Annual Report of the Town of Nahant for the Year ending February 28, 1863 (Lynn, MA, 1863).

The War of the Rebellion: a Compilation of the Official Records of the Union and Confederate Armies, 128 Volumes. Washington, DC. 1880.

Unpublished Sources

Affidavitt [*sic*] for Sophia Hood, December 19, 1902. "Elbridge and Sophia Hood" file, Nahant Historical Society.

Declaration for a Widow's Pension, Sophia Hood, January 31, 1902. "Elbridge and Sophia Hood" file, Nahant Historical Society.

Diary of Anna Jones Dunn Phillips, Nahant Historical Society.

Elbridge G. Hood Pension Request, copy at Nahant Historical Society.

General Affidavitt [*sic*] for Sophia Hood, Sept. 26, 1902. "Elbridge and Sophia Hood" file, Nahant Historical Society.

Letter to Edmund Johnson, "Johnson Family" file, Nahant Historical Society.

Letter to Joseph Wilson from George W. Creasy, Superintendent of the Soldiers' Home in Massachusetts, May 12, 1899. "Civil War Veteran: John Simpson" file, Nahant Historical Society.

Letter to Joseph Wilson from George W. Creasy, Superintendent of the Soldiers' Home in Massachusetts, Oct. 16, 1899. "Civil War Veteran: John Simpson" file, Nahant Historical Society.

Letter to Joseph Wilson from John G. B. Adams, President of the Board of Trustees of the Soldiers' Home in Massachusetts, Dec. 26, 1899. "Civil War Veteran: John Simpson" file, Nahant Historical Society.

Letter to Joseph Wilson from John G. B. Adams, President of the Board of Trustees of the Soldiers' Home in Massachusetts, Dec. 30, 1899. "Civil War Veteran: John Simpson" file, Nahant Historical Society.

Letter to Joseph Wilson from Commissioner of State Aid Charles W. Hastings, March 12, 1900. "Civil War Veteran: John Simpson" file, Nahant Historical Society.

Letter to Joseph Wilson from John G. B. Adams, President of the Board of Trustees of the Soldiers' Home in Massachusetts, March 29, 1900. "Civil War Veteran: John Simpson" file, Nahant Historical Society.

Letter to Joseph Wilson from Assistant Commissioner of State Aid Francis A Bicknell, May 4, 1900. "Civil War Veteran: John Simpson" file, Nahant Historical Society.

Letter to Joseph Wilson from John Simpson, May 23, 1900. "Civil War Veteran: John Simpson" file, Nahant Historical Society.

Letter to Joseph Wilson from Dr. W. E. Elwell, April 15, 1901. "Civil War Veteran: John Simpson" file, Nahant Historical Society.

Letter to Frank G. Philips from Dr. W. E. Elwell, Sept. 30, 1904. "Civil War Veteran: John Simpson" file, Nahant Historical Society.

Lynn, Massachusetts, GAR Hall, Member File Card for Elbridge G. Hood.

Mary A. P. Russell, "Past and Present from 1826–1911: Record of My Happy Life" (unpublished manuscript, Nahant Historical Society).

"Nahant: Civil War Veterans" file, NHS.

Nahant Historical Society and labeled "Soldiers Biographies" (hereafter cited as "Soldier Bio" file, NHS).

Nahant Veterans' Book, NHS.

Office of Commissioners of State Aid Returns, "Civil War Veterans' Widows: Ann Riley" file, Nahant Historical Society.

Pensioner Dropped, Department of the Interior, Feb. 25, 1913. "Elbridge and Sophia Hood" file, Nahant Historical Society.

Receipts, "Civil War Veteran Vouchers: John Simpson, 1867–1897" file, Nahant Historical Society.

"Richard Manning Hodges" file, Nahant Historical Society.

"Town of Nahant Memorial Day 1894" (Pamphlet, NHS).

Wilson Diary. Nahant Historical Society.

MISCELLANEOUS

List of Civil War Veterans buried in Greenlawn Cemetery by Philip Applin. Nahant Historical Society.

Photo of Baldwin Brown, Nahant Library.

INDEX

ABOUT THE AUTHOR

Steven C. Eames is a professor of history at Mount Ida College in Newton, Massachusetts. He received his PhD in American History at the University of New Hampshire in 1989. His primary area of research is the effect of war on soldiers and civilians in early America. His dissertation on warfare and provincial soldiers in New England during the early French and Indian wars is being revised for publication. He contributed numerous articles to *Colonial Wars of North America, 1512–1762: An Encyclopedia* (Garland Publishing, New York, NY, 1996) and recently contributed an article on Colonial Wars and Captivities to the *Encyclopedia of New England* (Yale University Press, New Haven, CT, 2005). He has had a lifelong interest in the Civil War, which has led him to write introductions to *The Civil War Diary of Lieut. J.E. Hodgkins* (Picton Press, Camden, ME, 1994) and the reprint of John Billings' *Hardtack and Coffee* (Corner House, Gansevoort, NY, 1996). Dr. Eames lives in Maine with his wife, Kathleen, and their three children.